CW01214982

BASINGSTOKE HISTORY
DELVING DEEPER ©

FASCINATING FACTS IN EASY TO READ CHAPTERS

By Ian Richards

Special thanks to Raz Razzle, Bob Clark and Dale Burgess for their valuable help in putting this book together.

First published in 2023 by P2D Books Ltd

© Ian Richards, 2023

The articles in this book were previously published in the Basingstoke Gazette Heritage and Flashback Thursday columns.

The right of Ian Richards to be identified as the Author of this work has been asserted in accordance with the Copyright, Designs and Patents Act 1988.

Cover design by Ian Richards. Photo The Holy Ghost ruins, Basingstoke.
Printed by Print2Demand P2D Books Ltd. Westoning, Bedfordshire, MK45 5LD www.p2dbooks.co.uk

All rights reserved. No part of this book may be reprinted or reproduced or utilised in any form or by any electronic, mechanical or other means, not known or hereafter invented, including photocopying and recording, or in any information storage or retrieval system, without the permission in writing from the Publishers.
Students, teachers and others using this site for educational purposes only, may do so in essays, dissertations or theses, providing that they include an appropriate acknowledgement quoting the copyright of Ian Richards and mention of the Basingstoke History Facebook site.

ISBN 978-1-914458-30-9

Contents

Introduction 6

Chapter 1	Ruth Ellis	....	7
Chapter 2	Blue Peter Retreads	....	10
Chapter 3	Tollgates and Milestones	....	14
Chapter 4	The Salvation Army Riots	....	19
Chapter 5	The Costello School	....	24
Chapter 6	Joices Waggons	....	27
Chapter 7	The Coaching Inns	....	30
Chapter 8	Education	....	33
Chapter 9	Hackwood House	....	39
Chapter 10	The Haymarket Theatre	....	42
Chapter 11	Mr Mulford	....	46
Chapter 12	Local Traders	....	50
Chapter 13	John May	....	53
Chapter 14	The Mays Brewery	....	56
Chapter 15	The Boys Brigade	....	61
Chapter 16	Alfie and Jesse Cole	....	63
Chapter 17	All Saints Church	....	69
Chapter 18	The 60s Pop Groups	....	73
Chapter 19	The Sarum Hill Centre	....	80
Chapter 20	Potters Lane	....	84
Chapter 21	The Fire Brigade	....	89
Chapter 22	The Candovers	....	91
Chapter 23	Lancaster the Explorer	....	99
Chapter 24	Lansing Bagnall	....	104
Chapter 25	The Quakers	....	109
Chapter 26	Captain Susan 'Hawker' Jones	....	114
Chapter 27	King Johns Castle	....	119
Chapter 28	Portals Mill	....	122
Chapter 29	The Basingstoke Canal	....	126
Chapter 30	The Shrubbery	....	132

Sources and Credits 136
Index 142

Introduction

As I have grown older I have discovered an interest in the changing face of the town of Basingstoke in Hampshire. Being old enough to remember first-hand the sleepy market town, with it's quaint streets and shops before the mass demolition of the mid 1960s. I remember, at the age of sixteen, the plans first being presented to the public in the *Hants & Berks Gazette* and, looking through the eyes of youth welcomed the new plans. An exciting new town centre with the facilities and shops that went with it was my idea of progress and I welcomed it.

Of course through the eyes of age, and hopefully wisdom, I have seen from a different angle what that entails. Yes, we have an exciting 'new' town centre, which continues to develop sixty years later with the addition of Festival Place, but I do wonder if somehow we have lost our birthright along the way.

I consider it a privilege to have lived through the changes. I remember vividly the tiny shops opening straight onto the pavements, the unique characters who ran those shops, the places we went for 'entertainment' and the journeys we took to find entertainment elsewhere when it was not available. The necessity of walking to the corner of the road to make a phone call and the frost inside the bedroom window when getting out of bed. Yes, I know some will say 'Oh get the violins out' or 'When I was a lad things were different' but they *were* different. It seems to me that all these things went hand-in-hand with the quiet market town that was Basingstoke.

Opinions will vary according to who you speak to in the street. Some will say that the town has been ravaged and destroyed, others will say it's for the better. I actually land somewhere in the middle. It's easy to look back through rose-tinted glasses and see the romantic scene as on the front of a Christmas card but we have to be realists and see that there were down sides also.

Whatever side of the fence you are on, I hope you enjoy reading these articles as much as I have enjoyed researching and writing them.

Ian Richards

Chapter 1

Ruth Ellis

Ruth Ellis is well known as the last woman to be executed in the UK for the murder of her lover David Blakely, but it's not well known that Ruth had connections with Basingstoke.

Ruth was born on 9th October 1926 in Rhyl, Wales. Her father, a cellist, made a good living playing for the silent movies. In the early 1920s he worked on ocean liners and became quite wealthy but due to the invention of sound movies he found himself out of work. The Grand Theatre (now the Haymarket Theatre) in Wote Street Basingstoke, still ran silent movies so, at the age of three, Ruth, along with her father, Arthur Neilson (previously Hornby), mother, sister and brothers moved to Basingstoke where her father continued his career in music.

Ruth Ellis

But soon the sound movies followed him to Basingstoke and Arthur found himself permanently out of work and the family's fortunes declined, until the family became destitute.

Arranged by Ruth's mother, Bertha, the family moved to rented accommodation in Bramley then on to Baughurst, Brimpton and Tadley. Local knowledge in Tadley believes that they lived in a cottage in the Newtown area. Bertha worked in Baughurst as a cook for the Stokes family at Inhurst where three ladies lived: Ellen Joe, Ellen Muriel and Ellen Sybil. Ruth's brother and sister went to school in Brimpton.

Following this the Hornbys moved to a cottage in Monk Sherborne, the children sleeping in a shepherds cote, then to a wooden chalet next to Park Prewett hospital.

When Ruth was nine her father secured a job at Park Prewett hospital as a book keeper and they lived in Dunsford Crescent, one of the houses allocated to employees of Park Prewett. In 1937 Arthur lost his job and, subsequently, his house too. Bertha secured a job at The Red Lion Inn in Basingstoke for six months, possibly living-in. 1938 found them living in 'a timbered cottage' in Sherfield-on-Loddon where Ruth attended the village school and then, aged 12, she moved to Fairfields School in Basingstoke.

Ruth in her modelling days

Arthur found a job as caretaker at Bradleys printing shop (location unknown) and after a short time, in 1941 when Ruth was 14, he left the Basingstoke area for London and his family followed. By the age of 25 Ruth had a son and a daughter, and by 27 she was in a relationship with David Blakeley, a racing driver. She worked as a hostess and a model to support her children, but jealousy led to the fatal evening of Easter Sunday 10th April 1955 when she waited for Blakeley outside the Magdela public house in Hampstead and shot him five times. He was pronounced dead on arrival at hospital.

The grave of Ruth Ellis.

Ruth was found guilty, sentenced to death and was hanged on 13th July 1955 at Holloway prison. Her body lies in St. Mary the Virgin church, Amersham, Bucks with the inscription 'Ruth Hornby 1926-1955'. The grave is now unmarked due to her son, Andy, destroying the headstone prior to his suicide in 1982.

Chapter 2

Blue Peter Retreads

The Moniton trading estate at Worting is a collection of small companies, some at the beginning of their lives, hoping to grow and become larger, repeating the history of what happened on this site in 1926 when Auto Tyre Services was formed, a small tyre company with dreams of becoming larger and more successful.

Blue Peter Retreads in the 1960s.

In time they grew and eventually became a leader in the country for the production of re-tread tyres, registering the company name of Blue Peter Retreads Ltd in 1951 from the name of one of the tyres they produced. The company expanded on the site and eventually took over the whole area, producing in the region of two thousand tyres a week. Like most companies of the time, Blue Peter had a thriving football team and also used to provide social activities for it's workforce and their families.

An Avon Tyre Company party 1948.

Blue Peter, although very successful, by it's nature was rather dirty and smelly. The smell of burning rubber from the buffing machines permeated throughout the building and it was usual to

Blue Peter FC 1963.

emerge at the end of the day black with rubber, especially from the Chemical Shop where the powdered constituents were mixed. Blue Peter was unique in that it compounded it's own rubber on the premises. Although protection was provided it was nowhere near today's strict regulations on the breathing in of harmful powders and, from this workshop especially, it was commonplace to emerge black from head to toe.

In the Mould Shop temperatures reached incredible levels in the height of Summer and workers had to work fast to service their row of moulds, all operated by steam, before once again being outside in the fresh air.

As well as car tyres Blue Peter also used to retread and repair large agricultural tyres in the Repair Shop. Inflated with large 'bags', these would occasionally burst at full pressure with an ear-splitting bang which echoed throughout the factory.

The Moniton Trading estate in 2016.

The production of steam did, however, have it's advantages in that a large reservoir of water was formed in the guise of a swimming pool open to the workers who enjoyed a one-and-a-quarter hour lunch break and made the most of the warm water, even in the Winter when snow was on the ground.

From the year 1938 an annual swimming contest took place between three Basingstoke companies, Kelvin Engineering, Auto Tyre Services and Thornycrofts with the prize called the KATT cup, named from an acronym of the company names.

Like any technology it is necessary to keep up with the latest trends and inventions, and also to keep the foothold in the market of the product that you created. This unfortunately Blue Peter did not do in both aspects. The company allowed the market to run on ahead as far as tyre advances were concerned, and they also allowed their production to be dominated by a large contract from Michelin which, when withdrawn,

A Blue Peter promotional badge.

caused the complete collapse of the company in the 1970s. But Blue Peter's demise has allowed smaller shoots of industry to emerge to go on to become tomorrow's large companies – completing the industrial cycle, and so, today, the Moniton Industrial Estate is a collection of smaller companies once again.

The Blue Peter Industrial Estate aerial view.

Chapter 3

Tollgates and Milestones

A Milestone marker at Kempshott, Basingstoke.

Way markers, otherwise known as Mileway stones or Milestones go back to ancient days to direct travellers from town to town.

Initially these were just piles of stones which later developed into more detailed standing stones, and these were the forerunners of today's signposts as seen on all roads throughout the country.

During the reign of Elizabeth I roads were in a bad state and the government implemented a method of raising money to address this problem. Landowners were required to contribute towards the repair of the roads within their area so boundaries were marked using mileway stones, one for each main point of the compass, and the landowners within these areas, controlled by the mayor, had to contribute to the upkeep of the roads.

Although this was successful in that it provided finance for the upkeep of the roads within urban areas it did not help the roads in rural areas which were in a very bad state. Due to the constant use of waggons with metal wheel rims, the ruts grew deeper making some roads almost impassable and progress was slow. So, in 1621, a bill was presented to Parliament for the establishment of toll houses on the entrance of towns, in this way travellers instead of landowners could be charged for using the road and pay towards the upkeep. Following this, in 1697, William III enforced the installation of way markers to direct travellers and drovers to the nearest market town.

Eventually turnpikes were created with toll booths. Turnpikes, (the term originating from the long sticks, or pikes, that blocked the way until a fee was paid), were eventually installed throughout the country to raise finances within the local areas. Franchises were created by auction for an annual fee (in the region of £360 pa) to enable local businessmen to profit from the tolls with the stipulation that milestones had to be erected nearby so that the traveller knew where he was, and the distance to the towns on the route. It was stipulated that these milestones had to be white with black lettering enabling the night traveller to read them by lantern. Unfortunately, income was often not sufficient to cover road repair costs and funds had to be contributed from government coffers to supplement toll income.

Basingstoke had several turnpike tolls monitoring major entrances to the town. Situated at Kempshott, Worting, Eastrop, Chapel Street (near the South View cemetery) and also The Kiosk Toll House situated at the entrance to the Memorial park on

A rutted road depiction of the 1700s.

Hackwood Road. Another example still in existence today is the rather unique 'round' house on the Reading Road at Chineham now a private residence.

Further out of town tolls existed at Dummer, Mapledurwell, Oakley, Overton, Newnham, Ashford Hill, Baughurst, Burghclere and Pamber, each one covering routes into Basingstoke.

In 1773 weighing machines were installed at Basingstoke and Stockbridge to check for overweight waggons. If found to be so, an extra charge was made.

The Toll House kiosk and The 'Round House' Tollhouse 2020.

Charges varied according to what the mode of transport was, in 1796 the fee of 3d was charged for horses and mules with an increased sum if they were drawing waggons with narrow wheels.

This increased in time to include droves of livestock. Only one payment had to be made in a twenty-four-hour period with proof of a previous entry in the form of a supplied ticket. Exemptions were allowed for members of the public attending church and soldiers on the march.

Occasionally turnpikes had to be moved to prevent travellers by-passing them by journeying across the downs.

In 1878 the turnpike trusts ceased, the concept not being financially viable due to the onset of the railways, leaving huge debts for the government of the day. Eventually all signs of their existence disappeared except for the occasional stone which can still be discovered hidden at roadsides amongst tall grass or weeds.

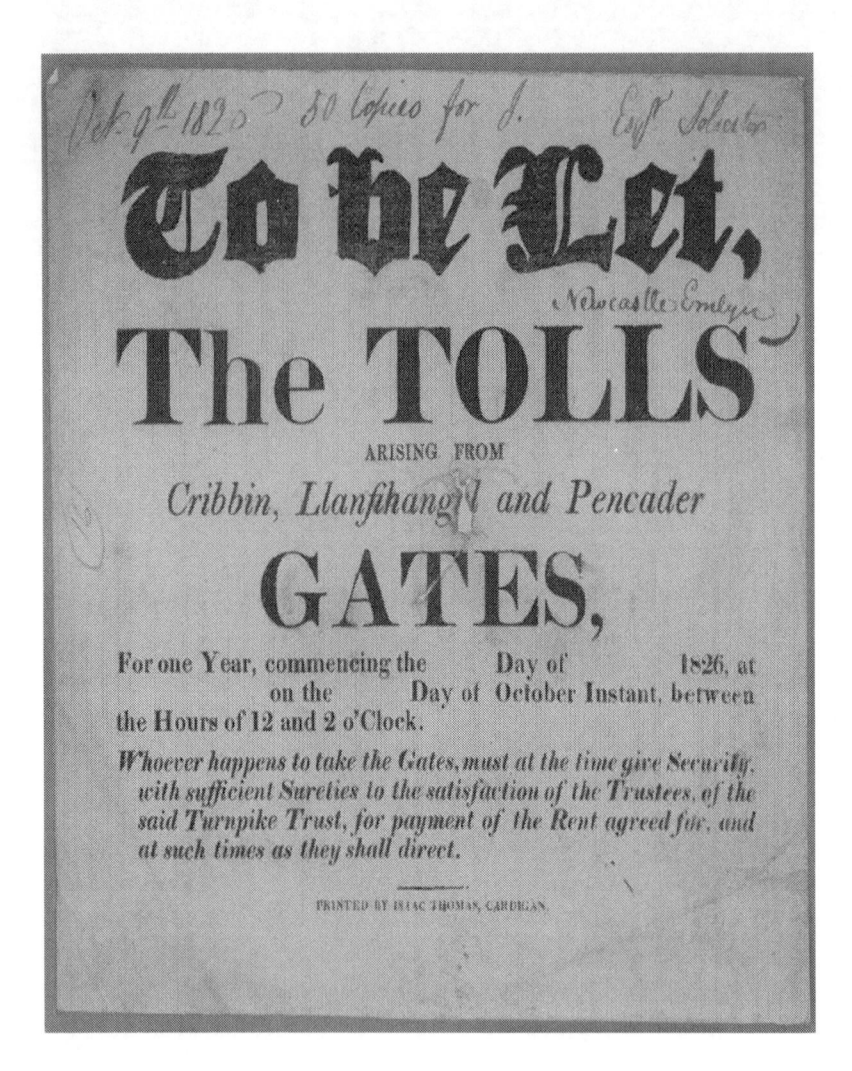

Advert for a toll franchise.

Chapter 4

The Salvation Army Riots

A major event that occurred in the history of Basingstoke was when the Salvation Army came to the town and tried to curb the alcoholic ways of the locals. It seems a rather risky thing to do. Basingstoke was a town with a population of just over 6,000 which housed in the region of 50 pubs and three breweries; and an organisation came in to preach against the evils of alcohol. That is exactly what happened in December 1880. The founder of the Salvation Army, General Booth, discovered that Basingstoke had a reputation for drunkenness and sent a team of 25 women and officers to the town. Perhaps not surprisingly the breweries did not take to it very kindly and strongly opposed them,

William and Catherine Booth.

especially the John May's brewery which was in Brook Street, just a few yards from the Salvation Army's base in the Old Silk Mill.

With the backing of the churches, town leaders and John Bird the founder of the *Hants & Berks Gazette* (now the *Basingstoke Gazette*), the Salvation Army grew bolder and held open-air meetings and services telling of the dangers of alcohol. This caused ill feeling, and skirmishes ensued until, in December of 1880, violence broke out with drunkenness a major factor. Stories of people being attacked, clubbed and ducked in the Basingstoke Canal shocked the local population. The timely arrival of the police saved Salvationist Captain Jordan from being attacked and thrown into the River Loddon at the bottom of Wote Street which, at that time, was several feet lower than the street.

Mr Soper's house in Vyne Road following the riots.

The diary of George Woodman recorded that on the morning of Sunday 20th March 1881 a mob of 200 people, armed with sticks, gathered in the Market Square in order to attack the Salvation Army procession. In a short while the numbers increased to 1,000 whilst those supporting the Salvation Army gathered at the head to protect them. These supporters were verbally attacked and pushed and windows were broken in Church Street. In the afternoon a drunken mob, who became known as The Massaganians, who modelled themselves on a London group known for objecting to the Temperance movement, gathered again and broke the ranks of the Salvation Army forcing them to collect in Church Square in Church Street where they then proceeded to attack them with sticks and kicks. A number of broken bones and injuries followed whilst the police and the Mayor, W. H. Blatch, who was himself a brewer, stood aside and watched the attack. Several local supporters were injured including the Rev Barron of the Congregational Church, now the URC.

The head of Basingstoke police, Superintendent Hibberd, made an application to the mayor for the recruitment of special constables and eventually on Sunday 27th March one hundred of the local people were inaugurated into the force. The same day the Salvation Armys' cavalcade was surrounded by constables as they gathered at the Silk Mill where the mob numbers had risen to 3,000. Later, as the Salvationists returned to the Silk

A shop in Station Hill during the riots.

Mill, the mob followed harassing them by singing obscene songs and generally being noisy and obstructive. Some of the special constables dropped out in fear of the mob. The Riot Act was read at the Town Hall and the Royal Horse Artillery were called in to clear the streets, some on foot and others on horseback.

The rioting became public knowledge throughout the country which raised questions in the House of Commons and a London newspaper reported that Basingstoke *"appears to be inhabited chiefly by a race of barbarians"*.

General Booth in Winton Square.

On 30th August 1881 twenty people appeared before magistrates on charges of assault and obstruction, and a group of Massaganians assembled causing disruption and threating one of the magistrates. Ten of the rioters were jailed for fourteen days in Winchester prison after which, returning to Basingstoke, they received a heroes welcome from their supporters with transport provided in a liveried carriage, outriders dressed in scarlet, and a band playing *Hail the Conquering Heroes*. The Corn Exchange building was booked for a banquet held to welcome the 'heroes' return, and the local brewers donated six barrels of beer named the Massaganians Slingo to the event.

The skirmishes did not cease as, buoyed up by the public support, the Massaganians won the 1st November local municipal elections. The celebrations from this success deteriorated into more riots and windows were smashed in the *Hants & Berks Gazette* office, the Congregational parsonage, the Salvation Armys' home at the Silk Mill and Mr. Sopers' house in Vyne Road the home of a leader of the Temperance movement, where every window was broken and an attempt was made to set the building alight.

Disturbances continued until 1882 when an attack was made on the Town Hall to release a prisoner who had been arrested for assaulting a police constable, and for six Salvation Army women who were thrown into the brook.

In time the local population became tired of the conflicts, the local breweries realised that the temperance people were not a threat to their trade and the protest dwindled. The Salvation Army quietly went about their daily lives after which General Booth visited the town, to much acclaim, to witness the building of a new Salvation Army hall, the first for the town.

Chapter 5

The Costello School

In Crossborough Hill, Eastrop stands a school building which most local people would remember from the sixties as the Girls' High School. But the history of this school goes back before the 1960s. In fact, the founding of this school was in 1908 in Brook House which was in long gone Brook Street, situated where Churchill Way is now.

The Brook House building consisted of four rooms on the ground floor which were used for classrooms and the headmistress, Miss Hinton's, sitting room. More classrooms were on the first floor and rooms used as laboratories in the attic. The Iron Room was in the garden which was used as a gym and an assembly room for the girls, about fifty in number.

Miss Costello.

In 1912 a new school was built amongst the open fields of Crossborough Hill, backing onto Basingstoke Common. Accommodating 120 pupils, the number was quickly reached and by 1968 the numbers reached more than six hundred.

Brook House.

Miss Hinton resigned as headmistress in 1915 and the role was filled by Miss Costello who remained in the post for twenty years. During her tenure temporary buildings were erected which became known as The Black Huts, and upon her retirement in 1935 the former pupils and staff presented the school with a portrait of Miss Costello which still hangs in the school.

The Harriot Costello school circa 1970.

In 1959 the house next door, owned by Mr and Mrs Weston, was purchased by the County Council and amalgamated into the school as classrooms for the Upper Sixth forms, becoming known as Weston House. As pupil numbers increased, space was once more a problem with pupils having to travel to The Shrubbery Girl's and Queen Mary's school, Basingstoke Technical College and Sarum Hill Domestic Science Centre, for laboratory and specialist classes, which necessitated a complicated programme of buses and taxis for transport. Obviously this could not continue and so in 1961 a large building project was initiated at the school adding a laboratory, assembly hall complete with stage, a kitchen, foyer and a gymnasium with changing rooms. Four acres of common land were utilised for playing fields. The following year, due to the generosity of parents, governors and friends, along with funds raised by the school, a swimming pool was added.

In 1972 the school was opened up to accept boys and renamed The Harriet Costello School, and in 2002 the school gained technology status; again renamed to The Costello Technology College but, on the 5th December the following year, a fire destroyed twelve classrooms in the technology and mathematics blocks. Following rebuild the new blocks were opened in 2007 in time for Centenary celebrations in 2008.

The Costello school today.

2012 saw the school converted to an academy with a change in uniform and another renaming to today's Costello School.

Chapter 6

Joice's Waggons

Halfway along the pedestrian area in Winchester Street from Market Square, nestled between the former Basingstoke Service Centre and Secret Garden, is an archway which leads to an insignificant car park beyond. Now known as Jacob's Yard in the days of horse-drawn transport this was a very important area, and where the car park is now situated there existed a major industry in the manufacture of horse-drawn waggons.

Joices yard circa 1880.

Because Basingstoke was a key point in the main route between towns like London, Salisbury, Southampton, Winchester and Poole, and lesser routes from Reading, Alton, Aldermaston and Kingsclere, it was ideally situated for the success of a manufacturer of waggons.

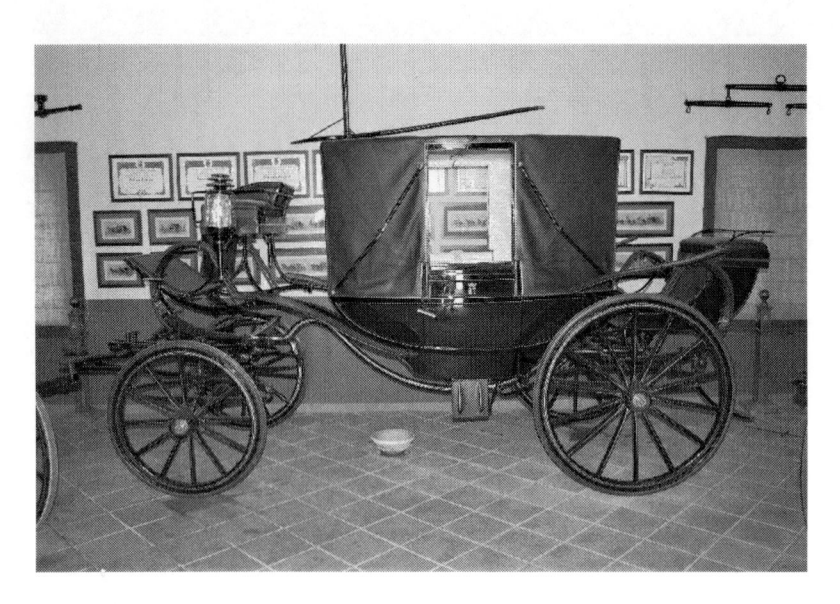

The Landau.

Joices yard 1967 – a painting by Diana Stanley.

Producing high quality coachwork and individual workmanship

28

John Joice & Son (Arnold Joice) was a leading name in the field with his waggons to be found all over the world. Recognised for their quality, each carriage was hand built in the finest Ash for it's strength, flexibility and lightness. Quality was paramount and a thing of beauty with the stylish finish of the wheels, shafts and accessories. Coach lamps were hand-made in brass with silver reflectors and crystal glass windows, and it was said that carriage doors closed perfectly with an almost inaudible click.

Arnold took over the running of the company at the end of the nineteenth century having served his time as an apprentice for five years in the Winchester Street premises, followed by two years in the Euston Road, London branch. It was reported that Arnold and his accomplice could build a Victoria carriage in eight days.

As well as being the manufacturer of waggons an income was also obtained by always being on hand when the stage-coaches came in from the various directions, a twenty-four hour seven day a week requirement of a farrier, harness-maker and wheelwright in case of breakages to allow a quick turn around for the coach to proceed and meet it's time schedule.

By the turn of the century Arnold was employing fifteen men and was producing a number of models from Broughams, retailed at £120, and Landaus, at £160. A miniature Shetland pony carriage was a speciality of the company and models were sold all over the world, including India. They also produced a one-off cart for two people to be drawn by the smallest Shetland pony of the time with a height of 71 cms.

Trade was profitable but was to be eventually compromised by the coming of the railway, the branch from Vauxhall being opened on 10th June 1839, and by the 1850s, the production of the first 'horse-less carriage' vehicles propelled by steam. This inevitably meant the era of the horse-pulled waggon was sadly consigned to history.

Chapter 7

The Coaching Inns

An important part of the heritage of Basingstoke were the methods of travel that existed in the past. With reliability on horse-drawn waggons and coaches the necessity for coaching inns was essential, and Basingstoke was no exception in the provision of these. No less than seven inns existed along the main through road of Winchester Street and London Street which passed through Basingstoke.

Day and night the sound of metal rimmed wheels rattling on cobbled streets filled the air occasionally interspersed with the sound of a trumpet announcing the arrival of an incoming coach.

The Wheatsheaf in Winton Square receiving the traffic from Andover, Salisbury and beyond via Sarum Hill, one coach being named The Salisbury Flying Machine which was proudly advertised as 'riding on steel springs'.

The Crown in Winchester Street, now the white building that housed the former Basingstoke Service Centre and The Secret Garden, was also an important coaching inn. The yard accessed by Windover Street housed the company of Joice & Son at the rear, the manufacturer of coaches. This area later became the workshops for Webber's Garage and is now a car park, but once one hundred horses were changed here in the course of a twenty-four hour period. A changeover of a team of horses could be made in less than three minutes. It was here on Friday 26th November 1798 that Jane Austen, aged 23, first arrived in Basingstoke with her father, following a gruelling four day journey from Ashford, Kent, including three night stops at Sittingbourne, Dartford and Staines.

The Red Lion in the 1960s.

Opposite The Willis museum at the Top of The Town, stood two coaching inns next door to each other either side of Caston's Walk. The Angel, now Barclays bank, and The George, now MacDonald's. The George receiving the heavy waggons from Taunton and Exeter, the approach heralded by the sound of bells. The Angel had a large courtyard and stables at the rear. Inside the arched entrance a row of seats allowed tradesmen to sit and wait for the possibility of work, drinking a draught and discussing the events of the day. It was said that an underground passage existed from The Angel to The Crown to allow late night revellers access to their carriages without getting muddy or accosted in the street.

The Feathers in Wote Street, still existing today, was the first hotel in Basingstoke, built in 1610 and believed to have medieval foundations. The name was associated with the heraldic badge of three feathers mounted on a gold coronet of the Prince of Wales Henry Frederick, the elder son of James VI and I, who died two years later aged 18.

The final coaching inn on the main street through Basingstoke is The Red Lion previously a tavern called The Three Mariners, which was razed to the ground in 1601 by a huge fire which destroyed a great number of medieval buildings in Winchester Street and London Street. The tavern was rebuilt two years later as a coaching inn and renamed The Red Lion, a name and a building that still stands today as a token of the long-gone days of Basingstoke.

Chapter 8

Education

Education today is an accepted thing. Universities are open to all who reach the required levels, and the path to reach that goal is well-worn, but it was not always that way and the route to gain education was hard-won. Just looking back to the 1960s it was accepted that the one who reached the heady goal of attending a university was very much the exception than the rule.

Fairfields school 1903.

Back at the end of the eighteenth century, education for the poor was thought unnecessary and was resisted by the upper classes as 'it would be prejudicial to their morals and their happiness'. This was stated by MP Davies Giddy. He continued that 'instead of making them good servants in agriculture and other laborious employments and teaching [the poorer classes] subordination, it would render them fractious and refractory'.

The British school Sarum Hill 1880.

Hence education for the masses was not immediately embraced by the authorities and provision was provided, albeit very basic, by the religious organisations, societies or individuals who had a heart for the poorer classes. This was not entirely benevolent, however, as it had been noted that new techniques in industry required a basic level of education.

The two main organisations were the British and Foreign Bible Society and the National Society, founded in 1810 and 1811 respectively, both centred round the teachings of the church. Both of these societies existed in Basingstoke, and in 1838 the British Schools formed an infant school in the United Reform Church in London Road (previously called the Congregational Church), and later in the Sarum Hill Centre, previously the Kings School and Baptist Church.

It continued to be that specific buildings were not provided for National School use so, from the 1860s through to the 1870s, classes were convened in the Vicarage, Church Cottage (next to St Michaels' church - known as the Malthouse) and the premises of the Richard Aldworth (Blue Coat) school which was in Cross Street. A statue now stands at the spot.

The Congregational Church, London Street circa 1900.

Initially there was no direct funding for these schools and debts grew. Parents were expected to pay 2 pence weekly for the first child and 1 penny for subsequent children. There was no obligation for the authorities to provide finances so the schools management took to raising money in other ways such as gaining income from property. This turned the tide and by 1877 reports were published that the schools were well equipped. By this time a total of 2,540 pupils were attending school in the Basingstoke area outstripping the facilities available and the decision was made to create a School Board which would enable the funding

St Johns School circa 1905.

from the Corporation rates. This was not well received by the public as it meant an increase in the rates required. What didn't help in the argument was that fact that the National Schools had allowed the existing provision to fall into disrepair and fail the expected standards by the inspectors.

However by 1885 a School Board was set up and foundations were laid at an area South of Basingstoke called Fair Fields, the site of pig and sheep fairs. This school would accommodate 1,300 children and be non-denominational which led one protester to state that it would be 'Godless'. Nevertheless Fairfields school opened in 1888, and the building which still stands and is in use today, is an example of Victorian construction.

This site was chosen because, being at a high point in the town, it was believed to be a healthy option for the children. Fees were still being charged until they were abolished in 1918.

Twenty one years later another Council school was opened in Lower Brook Street but this did not stop the rise of private schools for those who were able to pay more for their child's education. One school for 'young ladies' existed in Winton Square and

Church Cottage 1920.

The Blue Coat school building in the 1950s.

another in Soper Grove. A 'high-class boarding and day school' existed in Cliddesden Road and an 'establishment for young gentlemen' was In Flaxfield Road as well as the Queen Mary's School (then known as the Queen's school) which had Latin as one of it's subjects.

In 1901 St. John's school was opened which some older readers will remember attending. This was situated at the junction of Lower Church Street and Lower Brook Street on the site of the previous Hospital of St John, founded in 1261. St. John's school was demolished in 1966 as part of the new town centre construction.

The Basingstoke High School for Girls started life in Lower Brook Street in 1908 before a new premises was built in 1912 at Crossborough Hill, now called the Costello School after Miss Costello who was headmistress from 1915 to 1935.

Moving now into the more modern era, in 1960 the Charles Chute School for boys opened in Shooters Way, eventually to be amalgamated with Queen Mary's School (next door) in 1970 and the Charles Chute building demolished with the new amalgamation renamed The Vyne School. The name of Queen Mary's was transferred to the new sixth form premises in Cliddesden Road.

Chapter 9

Hackwood House

Behind a high wall on the way to Alton on the A339 to the South side of Basingstoke lies the Hackwood Estate, an area of 260 acres encompassing the grand building of Hackwood House just out of view from the main road.

This impressive house, built in the reign of James II in the late 1600s, has 24 bedrooms and 20 bathrooms and the main entrance is flanked by two gatehouses. The grounds include a botanical garden, a coach house and stables.

Hackwood House 1818.

The Hackwood Estate dates back to 1223 when it was owned by the manor of Eastrop and became a deer park. In the sixteenth century it was purchased by the 1st Marquess of Winchester Sir William Paulet, the first resident of Basing House and treasurer to Edward VI, Queen Mary and Elizabeth I.

George I stayed as a guest of Charles Paulet, the fifth Marquess, Duke of Bolton, on 28th August 1693, and the King presented the Duke with a statue of himself on horseback which was mounted on a pedestal outside the house.

Queen Elizabeth of the Belgians was given refuge during WW1 and King Albert of Belgium visited in 1920. In 1921 Sir Winston Churchill stayed on painting expeditions and Neville Chamberlain, following his notorious visit to Adolf Hitler in 1938, was also a guest.

Modern day Hackwood House.

In the 1930s it saw the occupancy of William Berry the 1st Viscount Camrose who moved his family from St James's Place in London to the newly acquired Hackwood House where he loved to entertain, but mostly he enjoyed the company of his family of eight children. At a young age William dreamed of owning a daily newspaper and in 1915 he purchased an ailing Sunday Times on borrowed money and turned it into a success. Based on this he purchased the Financial Times. His dream was realised when in

1927 he took over the Daily Telegraph, which was not in good shape, and, reducing the selling price from 2d to 1d, turned around it's fortunes doubling the circulation. The rest is history - and William became a very wealthy man.

During WW2 the house was used as a hospital for more than 16,500 Canadian troops housed in Nissan huts covering the front lawn.

Known to be kind to his staff, William was also generous to those he knew. Winston Churchill saw that side to him when, faced with the possibility of the sale of his home, Chartwell, Viscount Camrose arranged with his friends to help Winston to buy it so that he could live in it until his death in 1965, eleven years after that of Viscount Camrose himself.

Lady Camrose, Princess Joan Aly Khan, the mother of Aga Khan IV, continued to live there until her death in 1997. Now said to be the home of a foreign billionaire, the estate in 2016 was valued at £65 million becoming the most expensive country estate publicly for sale.

Still a magnificent building it stands as testimony to the wealth and prosperity of previous generations and should continue to do so into the future.

Chapter 10

The Haymarket Theatre

One of the most iconic buildings in Basingstoke is the Haymarket Theatre. Standing as a window into Basingstoke's past it was originally built as a corn exchange. Opened on 1st March 1865 at a cost of £4,000 it was purpose built for the time when the town was a livestock and agricultural market town. It was not an unusual sight to see cattle driven through the streets on the way

The corn exchange.

to or from the outlying fields. Reflecting this Cross Street used to be called Cow Cross Street, now a pedestrian area running from

Church Street through to New Road. In the sixteenth century Wote Street was previously known as Ote Street and later Oat Street, the word Wote being the obsolete word for Oat, but it certainly was not a pleasant road to traverse as it was rutted and muddy and not easily travelled by horse and cart.

The Haymarket Theatre pre 1992 renovations.

Great celebrations followed the grand opening of the Corn Exchange with a procession through the streets of four hundred people followed by two dinners and a ball, the latter which continued until 4am.

The Corn Exchange was sparsely furnished with only stalls for trading oats, barley, wheat and corn. Vegetables and soup were traded in the winter to the poorer classes from the Lesser Market next door in the form of an alleyway from Wote Street to Church Street, still in existence today.

Occasionally the building was used for public gatherings, as in 1880 when General Booth the founder of the Salvation Army held a rally and addressed his followers there.

Gradually as Basingstoke became more industrial the demand for use of the corn exchange grew less, and in 1910 the building's upper floor was converted into a roller-skating rink and below housed the fire engine.

Following a further change in 1913 the building became The Grand Exchange Cinema showing silent movies, (at which Ruth Ellis's father played his cello), and later sound movies.

The Lesser Market.   The Haymarket Theatre today.

In 1925 a fire almost destroyed the building after which it was rebuilt as a theatre and renamed The Grand, with a capacity of nearly six hundred people. With a further refurbishment in 1940 the theatre was taken over and run by Hammer Theatres Ltd who are well known for Hammer Films.

In 1951 the cinema was renamed the Haymarket, reflecting it's roots, by a local doctor Dr Radford Potter. Run by a volunteer group called the Haymakers, it was used mainly by amateur groups such as the Basingstoke Amateur Theatrical Society which still appear regularly today. In the early 1970s the theatre started to attract professional directors such as Guy Slater and leading performers such as Peter Cushing, Timothy West, Prunella Scales and a young Michael Ball.

Further renovations took place in 1983 and 1992 which produced the building you see today, creating a modern theatre whilst retaining the historic feel of the original building.

The Haymarket Theatre is still a centre of entertainment in the town complimenting The Anvil, a more modern theatre which seats 1,400, and will undoubtedly continue to be so for years to come.

Chapter 11

Mr Mulford

An interesting subject for these articles is the source of street names, some named after local people. The Berg estate roads Brackley, Pitman and Woodroffe are all named after Basingstoke mayors of the 17th century and a number of roads in the South Ham Extension of the 1960s were named after local casualties of

Mulfords Hill, Tadley.

WW2; Alliston, Burnaby, Butler and Dibley.
The Harrow Way estate took it's name from the route of the original Harrow Way which was trod by pilgrims visiting the tomb of Thomas Becket in Canterbury Cathedral, and it's roads Marriott,

Morley, Loggon and Lightfoot are named after early masters of the Holy Ghost school which was situated at the South View Cemetery.

Mulfords Hill, the main route through Tadley, also has an interesting history.

Mr John Mulford was a well-known character in the 1700s. Born in October 1720 he was a wealthy man, although it is not known how he came by his wealth. He was very proud to have come from a Traveller background and his relations were established in the Tadley area for many years. He sported a long white beard which

The resting place of John Mulford.

nearly reached his knees and he dressed in the most expensive clothing of the day. Although on a personal basis he was very frugal, being happy with just the essentials, he was very charitable to others, never rejecting anyone who needed financial help and generous to religious organisations after being influenced by the teachings of John Whitburn, a turf cutter.

He remained single all his life.

When asked about his ancestors he replied that they were 'Mole Catchers to William the Conqueror'.

The grave of John Mulford.

He was a fervent attendant of the local chapel and, during his lifetime, built two, including accommodation for the ministers. One in 1798 at Mortimer Common and the other in Basingstoke.

John Mulford's wish was that he would die suddenly which was realised when, on 7th January 1814, he died in his chair at the age of 94. This in itself is not remarkable but for the fact that the same morning he had said to a friend 'What a fine day for gossiping people to go about and say that Old Mulford is dead'.

He left £20,000 to be divided amongst his relatives and the church. He now lies in the graveyard of his church at Mortimer Common, next to his mentor John Whitburn, with the epitaph *'Gone to know more, adore more, love more; Christ Victorious,*

Satan Vanquished; Here earth take thy part of John Mulford', and now over two hundred years later, his name is remembered each time one travels through Tadley.

Chapter 12

Local Traders.

In looking at the historic past of Basingstoke it is natural to focus on the entrepreneurs and pioneers without giving credit to those ordinary people who struggled to survive with the little they had.

At the turn of the twentieth century and just a few years before the outbreak of WW1, twenty five percent of people in Basingstoke were living in poverty, children sharing an egg for breakfast, eating meat just once a week and families sitting down to a plate full of potatoes were normal life for many in the poorer classes. Women often made their underwear from rice or flour bags and some poor families made prams from orange boxes. Things were tight and the enterprising poor had to use initiative to survive. The first council houses were built around this time although they were not generally available until the late 1930s. In 1906 a Liberal government made some reforms and children were given free school meals, and in 1909 the first old age pensions of five shillings a week were introduced to people over the age of 70. Carriers travelling by horse and cart from outlying villages earned a living by taking shopping orders from people in outlying areas and travelling into Basingstoke, picking up orders for those who were unable to get to the shops themselves. Travelling on a recognised route each day of the week, some carriers took passengers maybe ten or twelve at a time, travelling into town from all directions on market days to buy and sell goods. Others travelled by foot or donkey. Besom broom makers from Tadley, an old man with vegetables from Little London travelling by pony-pulled wagon, women bringing fruit, vegetables, poultry, butter and eggs, selling apples, plums and red and black currants at 4d per gallon. Picking daffodils from Pamber Forest on the trek into

Chapel Street 1920.

Tadley Besom Broom Makers.

Basingstoke, bunching them up in neat groups to sell on the streets.

A well-known figure, Mrs Scamp from Pamber, would climb down from her cart and lead her donkey on the bridle down the long road of Chapel Hill from the double railway bridge selling her wares house to house. The neighbours learned of her arrival and would come to the door to see what she had to sell, and before long her baskets were empty, and she had enough money to buy her food for the week from the market stalls.

Gypsies were a common sight selling clothes-pegs or flowers in neat home-made baskets. Carriers continued in their trade into the 1960s when it started to die, along with that of street traders, due to more convenient travel and the

A knife sharpener.

increased frequency of buses allowing people to come and go easier and so another traditional way of life ceased.

Chapter 13

John May

The name of Lt Col John May was well known in the past as a major benefactor to the people of Basingstoke. Born in Church Street on 3rd June 1837, he became mayor for six terms, the first at the age of 46. He also inherited the brewing company John May & Co founded in 1751.

The brewery business, although very successful, was not John May's only claim to fame as he was a very generous benefactor to the town that gave him his wealth. A keen cricketer, he arranged for the All England team to play on an area he owned called The Folly, off Back Lane (now Bounty Road), later to be called May's Bounty in his honour, as was May Street, with nearly 200 houses, the longest street in Basingstoke before the redevelopment in the 1960s, and also May Place off London Road. May's Bounty became Hampshire's home cricket ground until 2000 when the club moved to The Ageas Bowl in West End near Southampton.

Lt Col John May.

John May lived at Hawkfield, now Bounty Rise, off Bounty Road. John followed the family tradition in that members were elected to the office of mayor of Basingstoke fifteen times between the dates of 1711 and 1839. Whilst mayor in 1887 he donated the clock tower to the Town Hall which is now the Willis museum. This stood above the town for 80 years until it was removed because it was deemed unsafe.

May Street in the 1960s.

Educated at Queen Mary's school, (in the grounds of the South View Cemetery in Chapel Hill), and later in Bracknell, Tunbridge Wells and Southampton, he eventually became interested in the troops leaving for the Crimean war. Persuaded not to follow by his mother he moved a resolution at the Town Hall to form the Basingstoke Corps of Hampshire Volunteers which he later joined. In 1864 he joined the Hampshire Militia where he quickly rose through the ranks to become an honorary lieutenant colonel.

The legacies left by John May were numerous. He built a drill hall at the top of Sarum Hill which later became the Plaza cinema, the space now occupied by the Sovereign building, and as mayor he laid one of the foundation stones of Fairfields school and another at the Lesser Market at the top of Wote Street next to the Haymarket theatre. He also held banquets at the Town Hall, was generous to the poor of the town and entertained school children,

The May family circa 1900.

at one event numbering 1,650. In later years he donated nine bells to All Saint's church in Southern Road, the tenor bell inscribed with the words *'To the Glory of God, John May gave me and my companions as a gift to this Church during the Great War of 1916'*.

John died in 1920 at the age of 83 in Portsmouth and his body was returned to Basingstoke for burial in the Chapel Hill cemetery.

Chapter 14

Mays Brewery

Although there were many small breweries that were serving the populace of Basingstoke in the earlier years the one that is remembered most is that of John May's. John May built up his business to eventually own many public houses in and around the Basingstoke area. The brewery, situated in Brook Street which ran approximately the route of Churchill Way West, was a large sprawling building and the rear stretched to the railway line where the company owned several houses occupied by the workers. That is well known, but a lot is not known about the history of the properties before they came part of the May group.

Dating back to the early eighteenth century there is mention of a Mr William Downs (or Downes) owning a small brewery in Basingstoke. There is not much known of this William Downs, but it is recorded that his wife was buried in Basingstoke on 17th June 1768. Their son, also William, died just after his 41st birthday two years after his mother, whilst in the office of Mayor for the second time.
William then succeeded in continuing to build his father's business to be a major brewer in the town. He did not come from Basingstoke, but was born in Shropshire and, at the age of 30, married Ann Tims at Hartley Wespall. In the maps of Basingstoke dated 1762, his brewery is shown as Mr Down's Garden in Frog Lane (the former name of Brook Street) now approximately the area of the Victory Roundabout.

Upon his death, on 7th November 1770, William was supplying nine inns and alehouses and was listed as owning an apple mill, cider press, a horse-mill for grinding malt, stock to the value of

£457 10 shillings, 47 pounds of hops and 305 barrels of beer. His wife Ann continued to run the business until 1772 when she married Rev William Paice, who then ran the business until 1783 when he leased the premises to Thomas and William May. The partnership between Thomas and William ended in 1788 and, in 1794, Thomas went on to buy the premises and the brewery renaming it May's Brewery. The May dynasty had started.

Hampshire being the principal hop growing county in the country meant there was a plentiful supply of hops for the brewing business and the May brewery was soon serving nine pubs in the Basingstoke area including The Blue Anchor, (the location unknown but believed to have been on the Western side of town), The Three Tuns (otherwise known as The Tun Tub situated on the corner of Winchester Street and Victoria Street), The Ship, (at the top of Church Street) and the Goat (at the junction of Goat Lane and Lower Wote Street).

Upon the retirement of Thomas, his sons, Thomas and Charles, purchased the freehold of the business and all its attributes, including the house and farm in Brook Street. He eventually was elected to the position of mayor eleven times between 1796 and 1836, and his brother, Charles, held the position twice.

Thomas May died on 4th June 1843 followed by Charles eight months later. Charles's son Charles Junior died three years prior to his father in 1841 at the age of forty. The business was then administered by Charles's eldest daughter, Jane, until 1857 when the brewery along with premises and sixty-three inns, including thirty free houses, from areas as far reaching as Winchester and Farnborough, were put up for auction valued at £41,625. However, the bids were not sufficient, and the lot was withdrawn. Charles's grandson, Thomas (1829 – 1870), was the natural heir and in 1860 he formed a partnership with his youngest brother John and the estate became known as Thomas & John May. Thomas May died ten years later and the same year a fire destroyed the malt house.

Mays brewery.

Mays brewery Brook Street.

The Cricketers Inn, May Street circa 1965, part of the Mays brewery.

Following the death of his brother, John then had to enlist two more partners, his brother-in-law Edmund Robertson and his chief brewer William Henry Blatch, the company then becoming John May & Co the name that became synonymous with the history of Basingstoke.

John May died in 1920 having built up an impressive number of nearly forty pubs in the town. In 1946 the business was sold to Simonds of Reading and four years later the brewery buildings were closed permanently before being demolished in 1966/7 as part of the town centre redevelopment.

The Goat Inn, Goat Lane circa 1960, part of the Mays brewery.

Chapter 15

The Boy's Brigade

The Boy's Brigade has for many years had a presence in Basingstoke. Active companies have been in the town since the mid 1950s and are still very much around today. An interdenominational Christian organisation, the Boy's Brigade, was founded by Sir William Alexander Smith in Glasgow on 4th October 1883, and has become a worldwide movement, working with millions of young people. Recent calculations stated a worldwide membership of over half a million boys across sixty countries, and over 50,000 young people aged between 5 and 18 in the UK and the Republic of Ireland in conjunction with over 1,400 churches.

The first Company in Basingstoke was formed in 1956 at the Sarum Hill Baptist church, which is now the Sarum Hill Centre and headquarters of the Basingstoke Community Churches. The captain of this early Company was Mr. Frank Strange and the founder officers supporting him were Leslie Richards and David Richardson. Captain Strange's wife also ran the first company of The Girl's Brigade at these premises. The pastor of the Baptist Church at that time was the Reverend Arthur Gove.

A few years later, following a disagreement with the church leadership, the Company moved up the road to the Trinity

Methodist church. In doing so the 1st Basingstoke Company became the 2nd and it continued to flourish for many years.

The boys of the 1st Basingstoke Boy's Brigade under the leadership of (L to R) David Richardson, Rev Arthur Gove, Captain Frank Strange and Leslie Richards.

The 3rd Basingstoke Company, which is still in existence, was formed on 12th January 1965 under the leadership of Captain Peter Waite, prior to this date the junior branch, The Life Boys, was formed as a forerunner. The company still meets regularly at St Andrews church, Western Way, South Ham.

Many children have benefitted from a grounding in The Boy's Brigade, with some going on to become officers themselves, and to form their own companies to teach and train the children of the future.

Chapter 16
Alfie and Jesse Cole

Jesse Cole senior and daughters.

Looking back to the 1960s one or two people come to mind who highlight the period and made an impression one way or another. One person who fits this profile is Romany Gypsy Alfie Cole along with his brother Jesse. Alfie was chiefly known at the time for his direct fight with the planning authorities to correct what he saw as an injustice.

Alfie Cole and pony.

Alfie's father, Jesse (Senior), married Emily Ayres in 1909, both part of a community who travelled Hampshire for generations before settling in Basingstoke, firstly in North Waltham and then in Holly Bush Lane, Baughurst. They had nine children, Freedom (Freda), Robert (Bobby), Henry, Louisa (Queeny), Gilbert (Gilly), Jane and Thomas (Tommy) as well as Alfie and Jesse (Junior). Louisa was the last to be born in a bender tent, or Vardo, which was a simple shelter made from willow or hazel branches and covered with tarpaulin.

Jesse traded in horses and wood from land in Old Basing, adding another site in the 1950s at Peatmoor Corner. The River Loddon ran through his land and he marketed this for fishing, to which the authorities at Hackwood Park protested and summonsed Jesse to court. However, the case was overturned due to the argument that

The Cole family at a family wedding 1950s.

the Hackwood Park estate only owned the centre of the river and not the shallows. In due course an agreement was made to swap this land for seven acres of marshland, where Eastrop Park is now situated, then overlooking the huge gasometers in Basing Road, visible across the town, which manufactured and supplied gas before the days of Natural Gas.

Using the clinkers from the Gas Works, Jesse built up a foundation to create a hard standing for parking caravans and this was soon used to house Romany families passing through the town.

Basingstoke fair, which was originally stationed at Stokes Yard in Brook Street, later moved to the Eastrop site, where it was often stored for winter months.

Jesse also used the site to buy and sell horses and trade in carting

The Cole caravan site, Eastrop circa 1960.

and wood, with him supplying horses to the Co-Operative Society, provided to him by Lushy Smith. Kindling wood was sold at twelve shillings and sixpence for one hundred bundles (62½p today).

By the mid 1950s the site was upgraded with a 'Change of Use' order to house eighty caravans with running water and toilets installed by family members. The Cole family also diverted part of the river Loddon to create more space. The site, managed by Tommy Cole, became known as Coles Yard.

Jesse's son, Alfie, later purchased more land next to Coles Yard and housed more caravans for the travelling community as well as a riding school but, in the 1960s, an act of Compulsory Purchase forced the Cole family from the site – but not before Alfie protested against the authorities in a way that has been remembered to this day. Appalled by the offer of only £7,000 for the whole ten-acre site, Alfie enlisted the aid of Charles Hemsley, a former Fleet Street reporter, to plan a headline hitting protest.

At 9.30am in May 1966 Alfie loaded his tipper lorry with topsoil and strategically blocked the whole of the town centre by placing four loads at key points, the first in front of the Town Hall (now the Willis Museum). This brought the whole of the town centre to a halt until the soil could be removed. He was arrested and fined £220 which he appealed stating that he was standing up for the ordinary person, but he lost.

Encouraged by overwhelming support from the public, Alfie then took his protest to the top of government by taking three days, led by Topsy his favourite pony, to trek to number ten Downing Street where, having narrowly missed Prime Minister Harold Wilson, he handed in a petition of thousands of signatures, a box of chocolates for Mrs Wilson and a gift of pipe tobacco for the Prime Minister.

The Basingstoke Gas Works circa 1955.

He also threatened to drive pigs into the Mayor's Banquet, which he did not do, but gained just as much publicity by allowing himself to be lifted and swung round by the 'world's smallest strong man' Ivan Karl at the local circus. Eventually, within a few hours of the deadline, the local authorities relented and increased the purchase price to £12,000 which was deemed enough for Alfie to sign the papers. His family moved out of the site and into local housing.

Three years later Alfie was again subjected to another Compulsory Purchase order for land to build Churchill Way East but this time the district valuer agreed to pay £36,000.

A bender tent.

Alfie, who was often seen in a local pub alongside his beloved pony, died in January 2021 aged 88 within a few weeks of his brother Tommy and Jesse's grandson Daryl, aged 30, signalling the end not only of a colourful local character, but also the end of an era in Basingstoke history.

By request from the Cole family this chapter was included in memory of Tommy, Alfie and Daryl Cole who passed away in 2021.

Chapter 17

All Saints Church

All Saints church which stands proudly at the South side of Basingstoke on the corner of Victoria Street and Southern Road has an interesting history. Due to the arrival of Thornycrofts, the industrial company producing heavy steam powered engines, and other industrial companies into Basingstoke around the close of the nineteenth century, a population increase put pressures on the local churches to accommodate an influx of new parishioners.

The laying of the foundation stone 1915.

St Michael's church in Church Street, the Mission Rooms in Reading Road and May Street were the only places that people could go for an Anglican service and it was widely acknowledged that there was a need for extra accommodation for worshippers.

At a parishioners meeting on the 9th April 1902 the Rev Cooper-Smith, the vicar of Basingstoke, revealed that his sisters had purchased a piece of land to the South of Basingstoke in Victoria Street which was available for the erection of an iron church. Investigations were made and an estimated cost of £1,000 was

An original design drawing.

assessed for the build. In due course erection went ahead and the church was completed in just a few months, after which a further appeal was made for extra funds to provide the fittings. This was soon met and the church was duly dedicated on Saturday 1st November 1902, All Saints Day, hence the name. The opening was conducted by the Bishop of South Tokyo, the Right Rev Doctor William Awdry as he was in England at the time. Rev Awdry was the uncle to Revd Wilbert Awdry the author of Thomas the Tank Engine books. All 130 seats in the new church were occupied and people crowded the aisle and entrance doorway when the procession arrived from St Michael's church for the dedication service.

With the thought in mind that the building was temporary and that there would need to be a more permanent structure in a few years, an All Saints Building Fund was set-up which took-off satisfactorily but then stalled and no progress was made for a number of years until 1910 when a fresh appeal was made.

The funds raised enabled an initial enlargement to be made to the building which added an extra 48 seats, but disputes arose as to whether the people were better served with a new church to the West of the town, supported by the fact that the May Street Mission had become inadequate to accommodate the populace, or to continue with a new build for All Saints. Eventually after much discussion, in 1914, a compromise was reached to raise funds for both churches. An initial donation of £5,000 for All Saints was made by Rev Alexander Hall, a retired priest, which enabled the project to go ahead. The architects plans were approved on 6th October 1914 and work started. The foundation stone was laid six months into the start of the build on 15th July 1915 by the Bishop of Winchester.

The completed All Saints church circa 1917.

The parish magazine kept track of progress as the building grew, and a mention was made of the donation of the peal of nine bells by John May, the owner of May's brewery. The Latin inscription on the tenor bell translating *'To the Glory of God, John May gave me and my companions as a gift to this Church during the Great War of 1916'*.

The final cost of the build was in the region of £18,000 the majority of which was found by Rev Hall.

The consecration of the new church was on Thursday 27th September 1917 following great pageantry and procession through the streets with attendance of members and dignitaries from religions across Basingstoke.

Chapter 18

The 60s Pop Groups

The 1960s are known to have been the time of the rise of popular music in the country with groups like The Beatles and the Rolling Stones among many others, taking the lead in the drive for supremacy.

In the early 1960s Basingstoke teenagers had to travel to The Gaumont Theatre in Southampton to see acts like Billy Fury, Cliff Richard and Joe Brown which was often out of reach financially. It might seem on the surface that Basingstoke did not take part in the early Pop scene but that would be far from the truth.

The Troggs 1966.

Many groups that have since become famous, cut their teeth in the clubs and venues of Basingstoke, promoted, no doubt, by the disc jockeys of the day, the most well known in the town being John Finden (aka Johnny Prince) who ran discos at numerous venues in the town such as Brinkletts centre in Winchester Road, which was also the home of The Basingstoke Youth Centre. These discos were known as the (short lived) Ticky Rick Club, Blue Room and Twist and Trad to mention just three. The Galaxy Club, who held 45 events in the town, was mainly based at the Town Hall before a limit was imposed on the numbers attending. Following this the organisation had various venues and supported many local groups as well as those more well known.

The Brinkletts Basingstoke Youth Centre 1964.

The Troggs from Andover with singer Reg Presley (Reg Ball) and originally called The Troglodytes, frequented the venues of Basingstoke as a support band in 1964 and 1965. They entered the charts in May 1966 with Wild Thing which reached number two, following up in July with their first number one, With A Girl Like You. The group was managed by Larry Page who also managed The Kinks.

Chris Farlowe (John Deighton), an ex-member of the John Henry Skiffle Group, transferred his interests to R&B and Rock 'n Roll and, following several 'misses', achieved his only number one with Out of Time in 1966, one of three hits in that year. Farlowe performed in The Haymarket Theatre Lounge in 1964 at an entry fee of 8/6 (Eight shillings and six pence).

Local group The Mimets.

Likewise Long John Baldry (named after his 6' 7" height), who appeared in The Town Hall (now the Willis Museum), in 1964 achieved his only number one in the charts Let The Heartaches Begin in 1967. His next 'hit' that reached number fifteen was Mexico the following year. He previously was a member of the Alexis Korner's Blues Incorporated and later formed the Hoochie Coochie Men. Following the breakup of this group he joined The Steampacket with Rod Stewart, Brian Auger and Julie Driscoll.

The world famous Who, with members Pete Townshend, Roger Daltry, John Entwistle and Keith Moon started life in Acton Grammar School in 1959 when the group The Confederates was formed by Townshend and Entwistle.

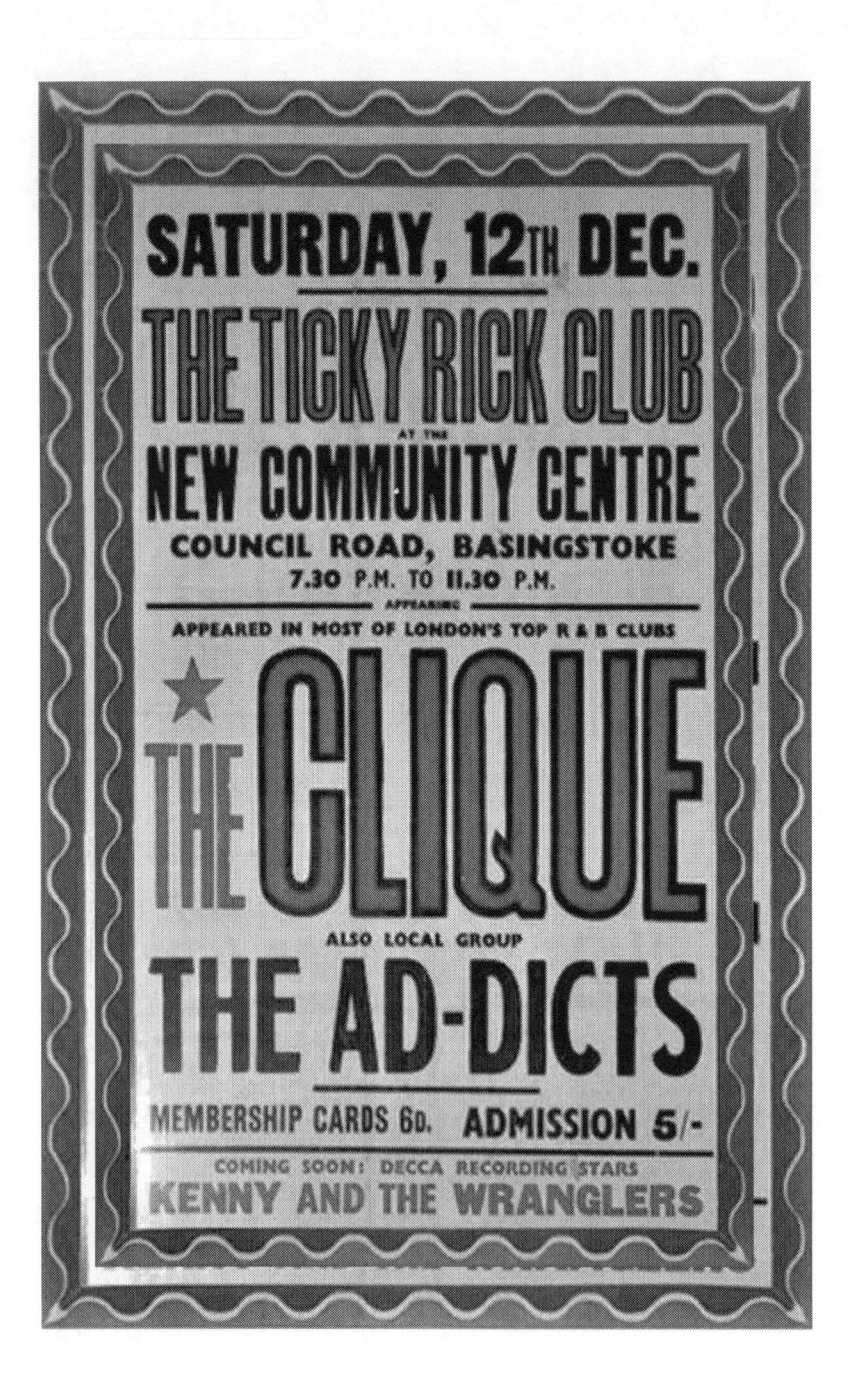

Advertisement for the Ticky Rick club circa 1962.

Georgie Fame and the Blue Flames.

They achieved their first entry I Can't Explain into the charts at number eight in 1965 and were booked to perform in The Town Hall the previous year but did not arrive, although they did perform in The Carnival Hall the same year as their chart entry. The first entry fee was 6/- (six shillings) but that increased to 12/6 (twelve shillings and six pence) in 1965, perhaps reflecting their popularity. Surprisingly Who did not achieve a number one over the twenty years they were in the charts, only reaching two number twos; My Generation in November 1965 (which remained in the charts for thirteen weeks), and I'm A Boy in September the following year. However, they did achieve fourteen 'hits' in the top ten between 1965 and 1981, the last being You Better You Bet.

There were also a number of groups that visited Basingstoke after they had risen to fame. The 'one hit wonder' Little Eva

The Pied Piper restaurant.

performed at The Town Hall in 1964 when the entrance fee was 5/- (five shillings) having made number two in the charts with Locomotion in 1962.

The Beatles at the Pied Piper 1967.

Also Georgie Fame (Clive Powell) and the Blue Flames, part of the Larry Parnes stable, The Yardbirds with five 'hits' in the top ten including For Your Love and Heart Full Of Soul, The Spencer Davis Group (two number ones – Keep On Running and Somebody Help Me), The Four Pennies (Juliet at number one), The Moody Blues (number one with Go Now), The Byrds (Mr Tambourine Man and All I Really Want to Do), The Small Faces (eight hits in the top ten with one number one – All Or Nothing) and The Animals (House Of The Rising Sun the only number one in eight hits) all appeared in 1964/65 at The Town Hall and St Joseph's Hall in Western Way, which was a very popular venue in the 1960s.

In 1966 Martha and The Vandellas and David Bowie appeared in Basingstoke, Bowie (David Robert Jones), three years before he achieved fame and reached number five in the charts with Space Oddity in 1969. He went on to gain twenty-three songs in the top ten with five number ones up to 1986. He died in January 2016 having suffered from cancer for 18 months.

St Josephs hall.

Stevie Wonder was also booked to appear but there is a difference of opinion as to whether he did actually perform in Basingstoke.

Although not having performed in Basingstoke one of the most historic visits made by a famous group is that of The Beatles stopping off at the Pied Piper restaurant in 1967, (when the 'Summer of love' and 'flower power' was at its height). Situated opposite the Stag and Hounds pub on the Winchester Road, the ground is now occupied by the Home Bargains store. A few months later John Lennon and Yoko Ono also called in for a visit.

The Anvil theatre, which opened in 1994, became a leading theatre in the South of England, and has continued to bring world famous acts and leading talent to the town, but those of us who experienced the heady and raw days of the live groups of the 60s will always think they were the best.

Chapter 19

The Sarum Hill Centre

The Sarum Hill Centre today.

The Sarum Hill Centre hides an interesting history.

Situated in the West of Basingstoke halfway down Sarum Hill, (Sarum being the original name for Salisbury), the present building was built in 1994. But the scenery was completely different in 1841 when the original building was built, isolated and surrounded by fields. It was built as a public school under the

Glasgow System of education, and, as opposed to the standard in England at that time, was unique in that it was designed to the specifications of the school master and it sported a covered playground, one large classroom measuring 50ft x 27ft and tiered seating for the pupils. These innovations were unheard of in the English System and were considered to be quite revolutionary. But within a short period of time the school was incorporated into the English System and had an attendance of over 120 children.

The centre as the Mazawattee Tea Company circa 1870.

Within 15 years the school was at it's capacity with 170 pupils, and a new classroom was added to accommodate these. In 1857 a charge was introduced for each pupil of between 3d (three old pence) and 9d a week.

Later in 1862 the Government introduced a 'Pay by results' scheme which allowed schools to receive funding in return for success, and In 1869 extensive alterations were made to the building including connection to the main water and sewerage system.

On the Southern end of Basingstoke was an area where pig and sheep fairs were held and it was here that was chosen for a new school to be built to house 1300 pupils. The area and the school were called Fair Fields and, although built in 1888, it still stands and is in use today. The site was chosen because, being at a high point in the town, it was believed to be a healthy option for the children.

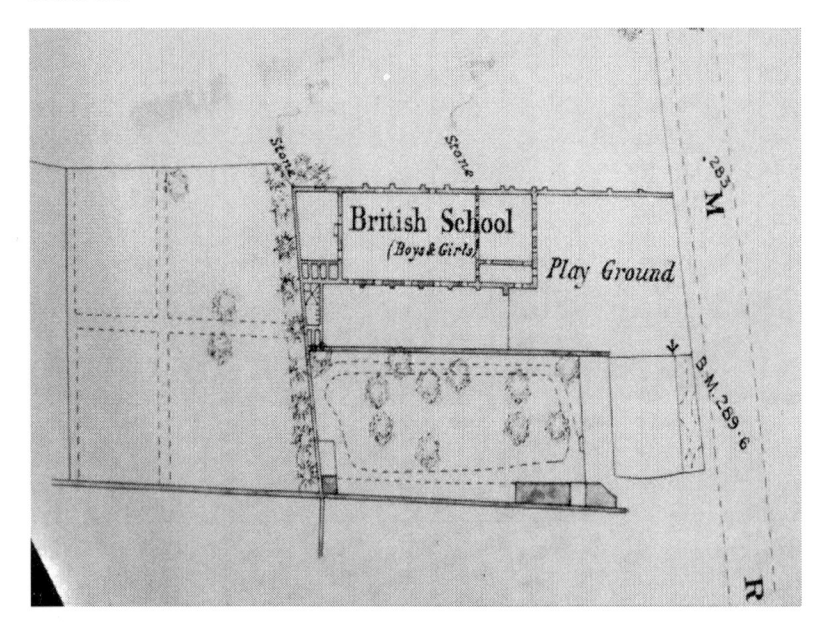

The original school floor plan circa 1841.

The building of the new school meant the closure of the Sarum Hill building which lay empty for some time after which Mr Wadmore (a local grocer of the Boro' Tea Mart situated at Gifford's Corner) used the building as a tea and wine store, hence the photo of the building showing the Mazawattee Tea title which was a very popular brand of tea from that period.

At the turn of the 20th century in 1908 the building was purchased by a Baptist group and converted into a chapel, and remained that way for the next sixty years up to the early 1970s when the Basingstoke Community Church took over residency.

The rebuilding of the premises in July 1994 was to allow accommodation for pupils of the Kings School, an enterprise created by the Basingstoke Community Churches group in 1982. The school was operating for 35 years but closed it's doors in 2017 reverting the use back to church premises.

In most of it's history the building has served the community in providing education and religious instruction to the people, and continues to do so.

Chapter 20

Potters Lane

When thoughts return to Old Basingstoke, one of the streets that conjures up the magic of those times is Potters Lane. It linked Church Street and Wote Street (situated approximately now through Iceland) and was named after a pottery that stood at the Wote Street end. It was a narrow street with buildings on both sides, the South and the North.

Potters Lane 1st November 1966 the start of the demolition of Basingstoke town centre.

The Rose and Crown, built in 1669, stood in Church Street and The Angel in Wote Street, previously named the Cross Keys, was built on the original site of the pottery.

Smugglers, en route to London, are said to have stored their contraband in Carpenter's Yard to the rear of the Potters Lane buildings.

A glass-fronted building on the South side, a former photographic studio, housed Southern Counties Cycle Co, a bicycle repair shop owned by Charlie Everett. Founded in 1910, his shop was originally at 35 Church Street until the 1920s when the business was moved to Potters Lane, a rather dark and dismal building which smelled of cycle grease and cycles hanging on meat hooks from the beams waiting for repair.

Charlie Everett's cycle shop.

At the Wote Street end on the South side, in the 1960s, was the Silver Star Chinese restaurant but previously this building was a café, coffee house and before this, the British Workman pub built in 1876.

The Philpotts bakery waiting for demolition.

Further along on the North side was Phillpotts, a baker and cake shop owned originally by Mrs Phillpott and her husband, a master baker, who moved to Basingstoke from Cookham in 1898. Mr Phillpott died in 1935 leaving his wife and three daughters, Winnie, Ruby and Gertie, to run the business which they did until 1964 until the closure in readiness for demolition.

Mrs Phillpott died in 1958. In 1898 Mr Phillpott created the famous Worlds Oldest Wedding Cake that stood encased in a glass dome in the shop window. This cake can now be viewed in the Willis museum. Ruby, who had a great sense of humour and was a proficient pianist, gave piano lessons in the room above the shop. A pile of Giles cartoon year books in the corner was an attraction which encouraged the pupils to arrive early for his or her lesson.

Gertie previously moved to Canada and, following the demolishment of the shop, Winnie and Ruby retired to 1 Beaconsfield Road. Winnie, who always had bad health, died in 1979 followed by Ruby two years later.

The worlds oldest wedding cake.

Ruby and Winnie Philpott

Potters Lane circa 1900.

Numerous trades were situated on Potters Lane over the years, from a corn store, Café, restaurant, blacksmith, leather works and grocers, hence the nickname of the 'street of many aromas'. Potters Lane was the first street to be demolished in November 1966 to start the rebuild of the town centre that we know today.

Potters Lane pre 1966.

Chapter 21

The Fire Brigade

In the days before the turn of the 20th century fire brigades were run by insurance companies who took on the role of protecting their members, recognised by metal plaques installed on the houses. This, of course, meant that anyone without the plaque was not protected in their hour of need.

By the turn of the twentieth century in Basingstoke, the fire brigade had become state run, but the facilities were still less than adequate. Prior to the invention of the steam pump the manually pumped fire tender was cumbersome and hard to manage and transport. Ten to twelve men were required each side to work the pump at five minute intervals after which another team had to take over.

When the steam pump was introduced it drastically reduced the manpower required.

A steam powered fire tender.

The fire station in Basingstoke was in the basement of the Corn Exchange at the top of Wote Street, now the Haymarket Theatre. This is where the fire tender was kept but the area did not allow for the stabling of the horses so they had to be brought in from other areas of the town, mainly at The Barge Inn which was situated at the bottom of Wote Street. If these were not available the search had to be undertaken to find other horses and bring them to the Corn Exchange which obviously took precious minutes. Almost comically when the alarm was raised a bell sounded at the Corn Exchange at which Percy Hopkins, the local confectioner, would produce his bugle and, day or night, walk the streets of Basingstoke alerting firemen who were not in range who then hastened to the Corn Exchange to prepare the pump for transport.

If the fire happened in the countryside a lot of time could elapse before the brigade arrived as the alarm had to be raised by telegram. This entailed a horse ride to the nearest Post Office, the telegram being sent to Basingstoke and another horse ride to the Corn Exchange. The fire tender, being prepared, the firemen then had to gallop to the fire. This exhausted the horses and it was reported at the time that, on sight of the fire, the horses were stopped for a few minutes to allow them to get their breath back. This would enable them to gallop in at full speed to make a grand entrance and eventually fight the fire - after a possible delay of up to an hour.

This was highlighted in a later comment at the fire of a large house in Cliddesden Road, on finding there were two small fires still burning when they arrived, one fireman commented to his mate 'Fred, we have come too quick!'.

Modern innovation has meant that fire-fighting is now an advanced technology but it should be acknowledged that all modern innovations start with small steps - and maybe hand pumped fire tenders.

Chapter 22

The Candovers

Part one - The Chilton Candover Underground Church

Travelling South of Basingstoke through Cliddesden on the B3046 you eventually reach the villages of the Candovers which are classed as being in an Area of Special Landscape Quality. Two of these villages house interesting historic features. The first is in the village of Chilton Candover. As you travel through the village, almost hidden behind the barns of Moon Roast, lies a rather

The church after excavation in 1932.

insignificant but attractive graveyard. At the rear of this is an intriguing, raised flint platform. This is the site known locally as the Buried Church. It is in fact just the crypt of what was previously the church of St Nicholas which fell into disrepair in

1845 and was demolished in 1878 leaving the crypt remains. In time this became completely hidden by earth and undergrowth and was only discovered when local man, William Spiers, recalled playing on the ruins as a child. Fascinated by the man's story Reverend Gough, the rector, decided to investigate and, in 1927, excavated the crypt which was still intact. It was then that the 12th century font, burial slab and stone tomb were also discovered. The slab's inscription *'Here lies John of Candover, God have mercy on his soul'* is believed to have been of John d'Andeley, a descendant of Richard d'Andeley who was the incumbent of the Manor of Chilton in 1086.

The crypt, tomb and font.

The original building dated from around 1100 but the first mention of the church was in 1291. In the 14th century a later church was built on the site when the Candovers were on the main route for The Oxdrove, the droving of livestock from the West country to Basingstoke and on to London.

In 1562 the owner was John Fyssher who mysteriously is recorded as being responsible for the 'depopulation of the village', the only existence of the village now being earthworks to the West of the ruin.

The church site today.

The manor changed hands several times until 1818 when it was bought by Alexander Baring who became Lord Ashburton. His family was key in the foundation of the Hong Kong trading house of Dent & Co which eventually became the Barings Bank, Baring Close in East Stratton acknowledging the family's importance locally as well as in London, Beaconsfield and Cowes in the Isle of Wight.

Each year a service is conducted at the crypt in order for it to maintain its consecrated status, the last one being on 6th June 2021.

The Candovers
Part two - St Marys church, Preston Candover

St Marys Church, Preston Candover.

Preston Candover lies on the B3046 on the Southern edge of the catchment area for the Basingstoke Gazette, and is not often mentioned as part of Basingstoke history, but I would like to highlight a particularly interesting small church in the heart of the

village. The Old Church of St Mary the Virgin, although at first glance seems to be a simple building, holds a number of surprises.

The floor itself dates to many earlier times. Flagstones, tiles and ledger stones were relocated when the original building was demolished in 1885, and used in the construction of the floor, including 32 medieval tiles. The majority of the floor memorials date from the 18th century and a brass memorial to Katherine Dabrigecort to 1607.

The South view.

An interesting feature is the memorial to Elizabeth Soper who is shown as having died in 1733/4 highlighting the difference in dates between the Julian calendar, (which Julian Caesar made official in 46BC), and the Gregorian calendar. Dates prior to 1752 were usually calculated to the Julian calendar which differed from the Gregorian. This caused a shift of a day every 128 years resulting in a huge disparity over a span of centuries.

The interior.

Because of this dates were often recorded with both calendars.

In 1851 the population of the village was recorded as being 524 and the old church as having 250 seats. Previously a fire in 1683 severely damaged the building and three restorations followed until 1872 when it was decided to abandon the old church and build a new one on higher ground which was completed in 1884.

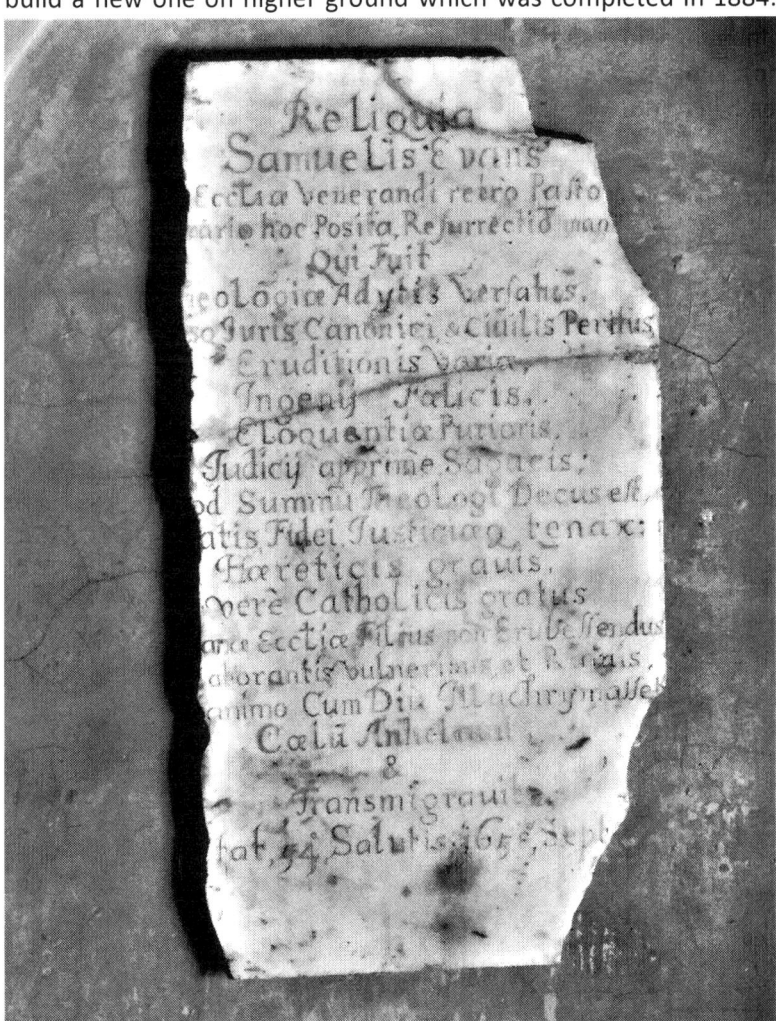

The 1658 commemorate of Samuel Evans.

Following part demolition in 1885 the old church was then used as a mortuary chapel with the west wall and doorway being added in place of the chancel arch, incorporating a fragment of a 13th century stone coffin lid and other interesting carved stones rescued from the original church. On the south side is a blocked priest's doorway and to left of this can be seen a mass dial which was used in medieval times to announce the times of the church services.

In 1984 the chapel was eventually designated as redundant and taken into the protection of the Redundant Churches Fund, which is now the Churches Conservation Trust.

There are many other points of interest in this fascinating building and a visit is recommended.

Chapter 23

Lancaster the Explorer

Sir James Lancaster.

Lancaster Road to the North of Basingstoke is in rather an innocuous area off Merton Road, but the road was not named after an innocuous or unimportant person, in fact the opposite, as Sir James Lancaster became a very eminent seafarer and was key in the formation of the East India Company, a trading link between Britain and the East Indies.

Lancaster Road.

James was born in Basingstoke around 1555 and, initially becoming a soldier, progressed to being a trader in Portugal.

By 1588 he had become a respected sailor and he served as a commander of the *Edward Bonaventure* under Sir Francis Drake against the Spanish Armada.

It was the *Edward Bonaventure* that he commanded when he set sail with a flotilla on 10th April 1591 from Plymouth on the first journey to the East Indies reaching Penang in June 1592. Pepper, spices, cotton and silk were the main trades of the company on one occasion returning to Britain with 500 tons of pepper on board.

Admiral James Lancaster was not known for being merciful when opportunities arose to increase the wealth of his country and those of Queen Elizabeth I. So when brought into contact with other trading ships, especially Spanish and Portuguese, wherever they may be, he thought it his duty to relieve them of their cargo, which he did on numerous occasions and filling his fleet 'to the gunnels' with bounty.

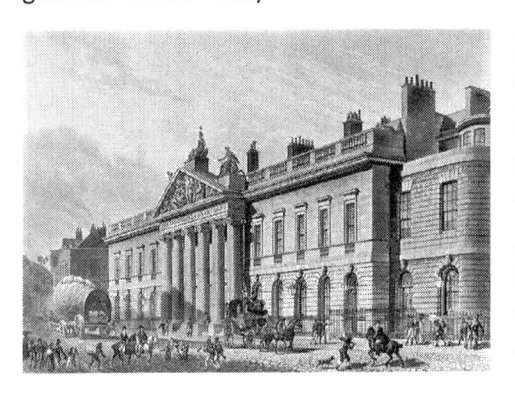

His journeys were not without their problems however, and if it were not for the quick thinking and skill of James on one occasion, his ship and its crew would have been lost to the sea.

East India House London c1817.

On a return journey to Britain in 1603 on board the *Red Dragon* a violent storm arose, and the strength of the sea tore off the rudder of his ship, which meant that it was in imminent danger of sinking. Thinking quickly James ordered that the carpenters on board fashion another rudder out of the mizzen mast which they duly did. This worked for a while, but the continuing relentless storm once again tore off the new rudder. Without hesitation James ordered another to be made. The most proficient divers were summoned to fix the article in place. This time the rudder held fast which saved the ship and its crew.

The name of Admiral James Lancaster is also connected to the fight against scurvy amongst the seamen which is still heeded today. Due to his observations he noticed that the taking of lemon juice, and other citrus juices, on a regular basis seemed to ward off the disease of scurvy. The disease caused by a lack of vitamin

C, causes listlessness, tiredness, sore limbs, gum disease and death, and was rife on the ships of that period to the degree that the ships could not maintain their daily routines and large numbers of sailors were lost. James regularly fed his crew with three spoonfuls of lemon juice each day with the result that his men were free of the debilitating disease and could therefore carry out their daily tasks. This was duly reported to the Admiralty, but it was a full 200 years in 1795, before they adopted the supply as standard practice, resulting in many deaths in the intervening years.

An English Galleon circa 1600.

Admiral Lancaster was a key figure in the establishment of the East India Company which, initially, was purely a trading organization. But this soon developed into a political body which ended up seizing and controlling much of the Indian Subcontinent, parts of South East Asia and Hong Kong. He remained as a director of the company for many years and was knighted in 1603. He died in London on the 6th June 1618.

Chapter 24

Lansing Bagnall

Along with the major industries of Basingstoke's past, Lansing Bagnall must be amongst the top. In it's time a manufacturer of fork-lift trucks, with it's well-known Pegasus 'mechanised muscle' trademark, known across the world, the largest manufacturer of electric industrial trucks in Europe, and an employer of 3,500 people.

The beginnings of the company date back to 1943 during the throes of WW2, in a small factory building in Isleworth and with a staff of just seven.

The Isleworth works 1947.

The merging of two small companies, J. E. Shay, (the combination of the two directors Emmanual Kaye and John R. Sharp), and Lansing Bagnall in 1940 creating the eventual company registration of Lansing Bagnall & Co Ltd. The works were in Little St Leonards in a converted school. As machine tools were of short supply due to the war, the company was forced to build their own capstan lathes from local patterns and 28 girl machinists were employed with the company on day shift.

Concerned with the lack of work when eventually the war ended, the company looked for new avenues in the movement of materials other than electric platform trucks and created the 'Imp' petrol-driven tractor which became a familiar sight on railway station platforms. Other electric and petrol-driven models soon followed in the form of platform and pallet trucks, and tractors and these were adopted for use on the dockyards. It is worth noting that there was no design department in these early days and the 'designs' were sketched on the workshop floor in chalk.

The model 'A' tractor was produced immediately after the end of WW2 and production of this model continued for twenty years. It's power was demonstrated by towing a Albion tank transporter complete with a Dodge lorry hitched to the back – a total load of 23 tons. This demonstration quickly swelled the order books with an order for fifty vehicles from the Ministry of Supply, and in the year of 1946 one hundred were built. The massive increase in production highlighted the fact that the existing premises in Little St Leonards were rapidly becoming inadequate and a search was made throughout the country to build a purpose-made factory. After considering sites in Wales, Durham and Northumberland the decision was made to build on a forty acre chalk down field off the Kingsclere Road in Basingstoke. However this was not plain sailing because, due to the shortage of steel and other materials during the war years, the Ministry of Supply revoked the building licence. An appeal was launched and was successful in having the decision overturned. This was extremely unusual in the circumstances and only one other appeal was successful.

The first turf for No 1 factory was cut in 1953 followed by factory No 2 in 1961. (No 1 factory later became the Electrical Assembly department).
When the factory was eventually up and running the new Model

'P' truck was launched which became the first powered pallet truck to be designed and built in Britain.

Basingstoke works Kingsclere Road 1952.

The revolutionary design of a shunt-wound motor and regenerative braking took the industrial world by storm at the first biennial Mechanical Handling Exhibition at Olympia in July 1948, but it was decided that the production of this vehicle had to wait for the completion of the Basingstoke premises due to the lack of production space.

The Basingstoke Borough Council, in it's part, provided twenty houses to accommodate the key members of staff and a shuttle service was run between Isleworth and Basingstoke. J.R. Sharp and the chief designer lived in a caravan on the plot, whilst other staff accommodated a corner of the new building.

From the early days of the company importance was put on keeping a friendly atmosphere and including management and staff in social functions. Soon after the move the Pegasus Sports and Social Club was formed and functions such as the annual Christmas dinner, annual Christmas party for children, dinners for long service staff and apprentices all were instigated. The annual cricket match between staff and employees was another function which was played on the company's own pitch as was the regular Pegasus football match. The Pegasus Happy Wanderers Camping Club was formed in 1976 and ran until 2023, regularly arranging rallies for caravanners and those having motor homes.

Product design building, Kimbell Road 1970.

A fireworks evening and open days were held regularly for the employees and their families which were the talk of families for many years later.

In 1958 three fork trucks were supplied to Shepperton Film Studios to be used in the making of the film *I'm All Right Jack* which starred Peter Sellers, Terry Thomas and Ian Carmichael. This was a clever advertising ploy because it put the name of Lansing Bagnall before people all over the world and soon regional depots were established in all corners of the Earth, including Australia.

CEO Emmanual Kaye was knighted in 1977. He was born in 1914 in Russia the eldest child of a wheat merchant and was educated at Richmond Hill school. He later took a job in a small engineering firm and studied at evening school at Twickenham. In 1946 he married Elizabeth Cutler and they had one son and two daughters.

In 1989 Lansing Bagnall was acquired by German company Linde AG and operated under the name of Linde Lansing. Emmanual Kaye became honorary president of Lansing Linde Ltd.

He also formed Kaye Enterprises Ltd which supported young entrepreneurs in ventures such as computer software and retirement homes.

Sir Emmanual Kaye died on February 28th 1999 in Basingstoke.

Now only a small part of the Lansing Bagnall site remains in the Linde Material Handling (UK) premises in Kimbell Road, the original site now covered by companies in the Knight Trade Park.

Chapter 25

The Quakers

In the early 1960s in Lower Wote Street stood a rather elegant building called Warren House. Standing back from the road with distinctive frontage and pillared doorway it held a certain elegant 'old world' charm even back then. This house, built by Quaker Charles Heath, sported a large dome over the original roof. The doors and windows were made of mahogany and the walls were solid.

Warren House a painting by Diana Stanley 1966.

Quakers or the Religious Society of Friends (or Friends Church) were founded about 1647 by George Fox and believed in peaceful principles in all walks of life. The movement soon created friction with the established church due to their non-observance of the recognised rules and rites. A visit was made by George Fox in 1657 whereupon he called the town 'A very rude place where they had formerly much abused friends'

During the ownership of Warren House by Charles Heath a plot of land next door was set aside for the building of the Quaker Meeting House, as previously the meetings were held in the Rose Inn on the corner of Brook Street and Chapel Street, although the reception by the landlord was equally as offensive as elsewhere.

During the ground clearance of this land in 1967, in preparation for the building of the new Basingstoke centre, many Quaker graves were unearthed dating from 1839 to 1954. These were transferred to the cemetery in Worting Road. The first to be moved in March 1967 was a lead-lined coffin which was untouched by the fact that it had been buried for 125 years. The photo from the *Hants & Berks Gazette* (the former name of the *Basingstoke Gazette*) shows the move taking place. A Mr. Martin wrote in the letters column of the same issue stating that he remembered seeing gravestones at the front of the building as far back as 1912.

The Quaker Meeting House a painting by Diana Stanley 1966.

Although there was a group in Basingstoke this was not the main centre for the Quaker movement in the area at that time because a large group existed in Baughurst next to Tadley on the Hampshire and Berkshire border, known to be the largest in Hampshire at that time. Friction was caused when a young man by the name of James Potter read a pamphlet written by George Fox in the local church causing the Rector, Edward Bentall, to throw James into the local gaol. From there he was transferred to the Assizes in Winchester where he was found guilty of reading the pamphlet and refusing the Oath of Abjuration which committed him to the recognised faith. He was sentenced to five years in Winchester prison then situated in Jewry Street.

Quakers.

At that time the Five Mile Act of 1665 was brought into force, which forbade any non-comformist religious group to meet within a five mile radius of a town. Baughurst, being outside the limits of Basingstoke, Newbury and Reading, was ideal for this and so the movement grew here. They were not without their problems though as James and his brother and sister, who lived in Brown's Farm, also were intimidated by the Rector and eventually James's sister Ann was also imprisoned for refusing to pay her church tithes. Cattle and goods were confiscated. He also tried to have James's brother Richard indicted but this failed and shortly after Edward Bentall left the Rectory.

By 1662 the numbers had increased to a level whereby a meeting house was needed and Brown's farm was adopted as the centre for worship, and a burial ground was designated in a field next to the farmhouse. With the installation of a Rector who was sympathetic to the Quakers plight, the numbers increased but this was not to last for long. Despite a secret visit by the founder George Fox a new Rector, William Woodward, came down hard on the local Quakers and sent the police in from Kingsclere to round them up, but they escaped by the fact that the meeting was held in the loft of the farmhouse. However he targetted the Quaker burial ground and arrested anyone attending. One woman was heard to pray out loud and was arrested for 'unlawful conventicle', sent to Reading prison and was fined by the seizure of her livestock and property. Despite a temporary relaxing of the laws by Charles II the victimisation continued and many others were imprisoned for their faith, including many in Basingstoke.

Charles II died in 1685 and two years later James II relaxed the law of the Five Mile Act and passed the Toleration Act. This allowed the Quakers to openly practise their faith and the meeting house in Basingstoke was reinstated.

Minor objections continued in the Baughurst area but in time the local population became respectful of the standards of the Quaker people and recognised that they were honest and hard-working.

Institutions such as Lloyds, Barclays and Friends Provident, manufacturers such as Clark Shoes, and confectioners Frys, Rowntree and Cadbury were all founded by Quakers and locally members of the Wallis and Steevens family were also Quakers.

Chapter 26

Captain Susan 'Hawker' Jones

In Chapter 16 I reported on the story of Alfie and Jessie Cole who were well known figures in Basingstoke in the 1960s. This article follows on from that with a woman who was an ancestor of the Cole family; an aunt to Jesse Cole Senior. Susan 'Hawker' Jones, a Romany Gypsy, was born and lived in North Waltham, the daughter of a rat-destroyer. She eked out a living hawking between Basingstoke and other towns selling goods and making what she could.

Captain Susan 'Hawker' Jones.

She was a rarity within the Romany community in that she could read and write, especially considering that she only had three months schooling when she was a small child and three weeks at the age of twelve, after which Susan made her own living by hawking. But she was fortunate in that she was taught by her mother, Diana Bull, who was very religious and keen to encourage her family to better themselves. Her father, although liking his drink, was also careful that his children were honest and pure. Susan's sister, Esther Jones, married Job Rawlings and lived in Windover Street, Basingstoke (now at the lower end of the Joice's Yard car park), and were involved in the Basingstoke Massaginan riots of 1881 (see chapter 4).

The Salvation Army Temple circa 1950s.

Unfortunately, Susan's hawking trade necessitated her to visit 'publics' (assumed to be public bars) and mix with undesirables where she could make a good living. This, though, led her to also take to alcohol on a regular basis, and she was often to be found drunk and disorderly especially following the death of her mother. However, after three or four years, on a visit to the Basingstoke Fair selling Brummagem (fake) jewellery, she noticed a troupe of Salvation Army songsters as they marched by, singing. These impressed Susan and reminded her of her mother's Christian beliefs so she enquired with them where they would be travelling to next and was told they would be at the Winchester Fair the next day.

Mrs Bramwell Booth.

Susan hawked her way to Winchester unfortunately stopping at a pub enroute where she was robbed whilst being drunk on beer laced with snuff. Feeling guilt for the way she was living and falling short of that of her mother, she began to avoid the company of those that would get her into bad habits, and to travel to the downs to pray and study her Bible. Searching for a chapel to attend, she was encouraged by her niece to try the Salvation Army 'barracks', (believed to be the Salvation Army chapel in Norn Hill, Basingstoke) where she immediately felt welcomed and she subsequently joined them.

Baughurst chapel today.

Susan went on to preach on street corners including outside the place where, not long before, she had been locked up for being drunk and disorderly. Going on she took every opportunity to preach to people and tell of her faith. Eventually she was transferred to Coventry and then Otley by the Army as a Lieutenant, always having a heart and concern for people that were rejected and downtrodden; seeing many converted to

Christianity, one being a woman who had sold her daughters for alcohol. Moving on to Todmorden and Keighley she visited the streets of brothels and gained the respect of prostitutes, influencing them towards her faith, which did not go down well with the keepers. Whilst in Warrington for seven months she saw in the region of one thousand converts.

Finally, she was posted to Colchester and worked with Mrs Bramwell Booth, the daughter-in-law of William Booth the founder of the Salvation Army.

St Stephen's Church, Baughurst.

Following a visit to Canada Susan retired from active service to her home in Baughurst and, being in much demand throughout the area, held revival services at the Baughurst Primitive Methodist Chapel, (built in 1872, now a private home).

Captain Susan 'Hawker' Jones died peacefully in the Spring of 1892 and her burial took place at St Stephen's Church, Baughurst on

22nd April 1892 where she was interred alongside the graves of her parents, the positions not known. The inscription on her gravestone read *'Once a hawker, then captain of the Salvation Army, a good soldier of Jesus Christ.'*

The War Cry paper obituary 14th May 1892.

Chapter 27
King John's Castle

Take a stroll along the quiet and peaceful bank of the Basingstoke Canal at Odiham not far from Basingstoke and you happen across the ruin of an ancient castle. Quietly nestled within a small clearing amongst the trees it is easy to consider that this ruin is of no real significance. In fact the ruin of Odiham castle, known locally as Kings John's castle, was a key point in history when King John was on the English throne. Ruling from 27 May 1199 – 19 October 1216 his was a reign which saw the foundations laid for the future of Britain and the fairness of society.

King John's castle 2018.

John inherited the English throne on the death of his older brother Richard I, known as Richard the Lionheart, as the third king in the

House of the Plantagenet. He was nicknamed John Lackland because he was not expected to inherit lands of any significance.

King John's castle was built around 1207 of flint and timber and lime mortar, in about twenty acres of land at an estimated cost of £10,000. It had a two-storey keep and a square moat and notably a King's house. The only part left today is the octagonal keep and surrounding earthworks.

It was from this castle that it is believed that John left on the morning of 15th June 1215 to journey to Runnymede near Windsor for the historic signing of the Magna Carta (or the Great Charter).

King John.

The King's relationship with his people was as turbulent as his personal life and this led to problems with the landowners who were in debt to the King. The Magna Carta was drafted by the Archbishop of Canterbury to try to settle the conflicts between the King and his subjects, but it soon became apparent that both the King and his Barons had no intention of sticking to the agreements they had made, which caused friction eventually leading to civil war aided by French army under the leadership of Louis VIII. Eventually the agreement was redrafted which resulted in the protection of church rights, illegal imprisonment, limits on the payments to the Crown and faster justice for the barons which then became acceptable for both sides.

Over his reign King John lost most of his French lands to Phillip II of France and the Duchy of Normandy. Depicted as a cruel, petty and vindictive man he has become a figure of the villain in modern films and stories such as the Robin Hood sagas.

The Magna Carta 1215.

As in many ancient monuments, the castle is also reputed to have it's own ghost, which sings an ancient song accompanied by a lute.

In 1792 part of the castle grounds were destroyed by the digging of the Basingstoke Canal.

Only four copies of the original Magna Carta survive, one of which is on view in Salisbury Cathedral. An attempt to steal this rare document was made by Mark Royden on October 25, 2018.

Chapter 28

Portals Mill

In 2022 the announcement was made in the media that security printer, Portals, in Overton is to close, and this chapter is to acknowledge the history of this iconic company.

Frenchman Henri Portal founded the company in 1712 at Bere Mill near Whitchurch following an apprenticeship at a paper making company near Southampton; *The White Paper Makers Company of England*. Henry soon acquired the business acumen to follow

Laverstoke people waiting for the royal visit April 1923.

new technology and leads and secured a contract with the Bank of England to manufacture bank notes, eventually moving to Laverstoke Mill (at the time of writing the home of Bombay

Sapphire Gin).

In 1809 he opened Bathford Mill in Somerset which continues to manufacture security papers to this day.

King George V visit Portals 1923.

The coming of the railway from London to Southampton in 1840, led to the building of Overton Mill alongside the Overton railway station. A siding was included to transport coal and paper and twelve bungalows were built for workers. This increased access along with productivity.

In the early years the majority of staff were from the surrounding area but the railway allowed people from further away to be employed, which I personally witnessed in the early 1960s when, weekday mornings and afternoons, many women boarded the steam trains at Basingstoke station for Overton and back, when I was briefly employed by W.H. Smith on the bookstall on Platform One. (The only remaining signs of the bookstall today being marks on the brickwork).

In 1923 King George V and Queen Mary visited the mill followed by King George VI and Queen Elizabeth the Queen Mother in 1938. The late Queen Elizabeth II also made a visit in 1963.

Overton Mill today.

During WW2, the Bank of England used an underground vault at Overton to store its printing plant to avoid attacks by the enemy.

In 1940 Portals printed the first bank notes with metal security threads, included in the new issues of the £1 and ten shilling notes. The watermark highlights were introduced in the 1970s.

Portals increased production, eventually supplying security paper to over one hundred countries and enough paper to make 12 billion bank notes a year from the Overton Mill.

At the breakout of WW1 Portals were employing 359 people, which in the 1960s increased to a staggering 1,550 before automation reduced the figure. In 1968 about 150 were made redundant with a temporary lull in production. Today the figure stands at just over three hundred with the ability to produce 14,000 tonnes of banknote paper a year. The returns to the end of the fiscal year of 2020/21 showed a sales figure of £121.8 million but, after being acquired by De La Rue in 1995, the withdrawal of a large contract by them severely affected the total output of the company. Eventually the company was sold by De La Rue in 2018 and the name of Portals was re-instated.

The announcement of the closure of Portals at Overton, although the Bathford Mill will remain open, marks the end of a very long era for the area, a total of three hundred years.

Chapter 29

The Basingstoke Canal

The building of the Basingstoke Canal was an incredible feat of engineering, stretching more than 31 miles from Weybridge to Basingstoke moving thousands of tons of soil and constructing 29 locks with a workforce of over 100 men, working with picks and shovels; but it was also a story of incompetence and ineptitude.

The initial plan of the canal was authorised by royal assent and governmental approval on the 15 May 1778 and the Basingstoke Navigation Company was formed with shares to the value of £86,000. The first meeting of the Basingstoke Navigation Company was at the Crown Inn in Basingstoke where agreement was reached with caveats. The canal could not be dug through anyone's yard, park or paddock, and that no water could be taken from the River Loddon due to the demand needed to power the mills on the river.

The Act also imposed a maximum tonnage rate on goods of 1 1/2 (old) pence per ton if the canal was built around Tylney Hall at Rotherwick or 2 pence if built through Greywell; eventually the Greywell route was agreed by cutting straight through a hill.

In 1787 William Jessop, a well known canal builder of his day, was appointed surveyor and John Pinkerton was awarded the main contract, Pinkertons being the largest firm of early canal builders. The dig began in October 1788, late due to problems raising finances, and continued only stopping for the Winter period when the soil was frozen.

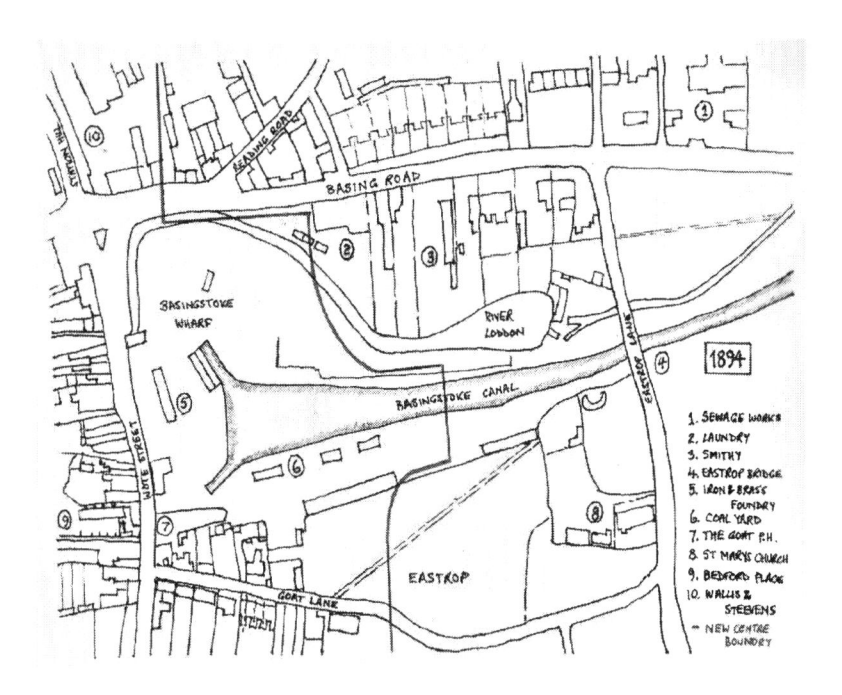

The plan of Basingstoke wharf from 1894 showing the extent of the new shopping centre.

At Pirbright the cut necessitated the raising of the level by 29.5 metres which in turn made it necessary to install fourteen locks within a distance of two miles. This involved digging a cutting of over 21 metres deep - after which the area became known as Deepcut.

The canal was to be the main artery for transporting heavy goods winding it's way through Woking, Brookwood, Pirbright, Dogmersfield, Winchfield and Odiham. From Odiham it travelled past the site of King John's Castle and through the Greywell tunnel which, at 1,120 metres in length and 42 metres below the surface, was the 12th longest canal tunnel in the country. After the tunnel the canal wound past Up Nately and Basing House and into Basingstoke wharf at the bottom of Wote Street approximately where Potters Walk is now.

The entrance to the tunnel at Greywell.

Things did not run smoothly however as sub-contractor Charles Jones, a mason and miner, was employed to build the Greywell tunnel. On a previous project on the Shepperton tunnel build on the Thames & Severn Canal, Charles's ineptitude and dishonesty became apparent and he was arrested three times and sent to prison for debts. At one point this tunnel collapsed under his supervision, but that didn't prevent him from securing the Greywell Tunnel contract. Inevitably this did not go well because he continued in his ways and was caught in 'improper conduct', possibly inebriation, and Pinkerton decided that once the tunnel was completed he should be sacked.

Richard Hudson, another sub-contractor, absconded with the workers wages and the Pinkerton company had to bail them out after which the company requested the workers select their own foreman to avoid a similar situation happening again.

During the excavation a Saxon idol was unearthed and, at Basing

House, 800 golden guineas were discovered by a local watchmaker, possibly buried during Oliver Cromwell's siege in 1645.

In August 1789 it was discovered that 161,000 bricks had been badly made and could not be used and had to be removed. (Fifteen years later lock walls and wings had to be replaced due to the faulty bricks). During the same year due to the shortage of coinage countrywide, Pinkertons produced their own copper and silver tokens in order to pay their workers which were accepted locally in the shops and pubs, one being the George at Odiham. Some of these tokens can be seen today in the Willis museum.

The canal was completed on 4 September 1794.

Basingstoke wharf 1904.

Various people paid rent for use of the canal such as the Hampshire Brick & Tile Company paying £40 a year to be able to wharf at Basingstoke, The Surrey County Asylum paid £10 per annum for water, and The Gospel Mission paid twenty shillings a year to be allowed to preach from Ash Wharf.

As well as being used for commercial purposes the canal also served as a water supply when fires broke out in the town. On Monday 17th April 1905 the Burberry department store in Winchester Street was ablaze. The fire raged for three days and the demand for water was so great that the fire brigade ran hoses from the canal to Winchester Street via Potters Lane, Cross Street and New Street, a distance of about half a mile.

The canal was regularly used as recreation when frozen over and skaters enjoyed the thick ice as in February 1855 when Samuel Attwood reported that he 'went sliding six times on the Basingstoke Canal.'*

Like most innovations they have their time for a while and then fade as new inventions take their place and this was the case in the life of the canal. The coming of the railway meant easier and faster transportation of goods and this reflected on the use and therefore the financial viability of the canal. It was never as profitable as predicted and shareholders began to desert their investments as trade began to dry up. Also damage was caused by the soldiers at Aldershot Army Camp and added to this the company's barge, Horsham, sunk with it's full cargo of coal and a court case ensued in which the contractor was sued for £200 for the loss of his cargo.

Eventually the coal supply to Aldershot Camp, previously transported by barge, was transferred to rail, followed by the horse manure supply.

In December 1865, at a meeting held in the Grays Inn Coffee House in Holborn, the decision was made to close the canal as a business venture, and the following June an order was raised to wind up the Basingstoke Navigation Company. Other speculators tried to revive the life of the canal which ultimately failed and The

Hampshire Brick & Tile Company also went into liquidation in 1901 after efforts to keep them as a viable business.

The Greywell tunnel collapsed in 1932, became a home for Natterrers bats, and traces of the canal to Basingstoke slowly disappeared.

In the early 1960s the Basingstoke Canal Society was formed to preserve and restore parts of the canal which continues today.

Although most of the length of the canal still exists any trace of it's existence approaching Basingstoke have been lost, as has much of the small market town that once was Basingstoke, for better or worse is a matter of opinion.

Chapter 30

The Shrubbery

Anyone who lived in the Basingstoke area in the 1960s and 70s will remember the large building in Cliddesden Road known as The Shrubbery Maternity Home, majestically standing back off the road with a long drive surrounded by Rhododendron bushes. But this is only part of the story. The Shrubbery was built in 1830 during the rein of William IV. It was originally owned by Joseph Wood of Sherborne St John but after a few short years it was purchased by surgeon Edward Covey. Edward and his wife Jane had six children but Jane died in 1851, and rumour says that the ghost of Jane roamed the house in latter years. Edward himself died in 1861 after which the property passed to Thomas May.

The Shrubbery circa 1930.

Thomas was a magistrate and a relation of the town's benefactor Lieutenant Colonel John May (see chapter 13). He only lived in the house for four years before selling it to William Henry Fryer and his wife Jessie Jane.

The Mother and baby statue.

He was a solicitor, but died at the age of 49 in 1874. Jessie remarried Alfred Charles, a relation of William who was a Lieutenant in Queen Victoria's Foot Regiment. He went on to become a Lieutenant Colonel.

Following ownership by other families the next recognisable name to purchase the property was Thomas Burberry in 1909. Thomas was the founder of the Burberry wax raincoat created in Basingstoke and now world famous. Although this was owned by Thomas senior it was his son Thomas Newman Burberry who lived there. He had seven children. Under the tenancy of Thomas the Shrubbery saw several alterations to the building.

The Shrubbery in the 1960s.

Nearly twenty years after Thomas's death in 1926, his widow sold the house to the Basingstoke Council for use as a maternity home which opened in 1947, presided over by the first matron Welshwoman Beatrice Bainton (and her dog Peter) who held the role until 1965 when she retired. 'Sister (Jessie) Jack' worked alongside Matron Bainton for the years she was matron and beyond until the maternity home ceased in 1974. A statue of

Mother and Child stood in the entrance hall for the length of time the home was open after which it was transferred to the Maternity wing of the Basingstoke and District Hospital. In September 1950, only three years after the opening, baby Valerie Diane Andrews became a celebrity as the 1000th baby to be born at the premises and a presentation of a silver spoon was made to her by the Mayor.

Following a period where The Shrubbery fell into disrepair it was eventually converted into an arts centre and The Horseshoe Theatre Company took residence under the leadership of Guy Slater. The group was in residence until 1989 when a fire damaged the building. Following some restoration, the building continued to be in use by the Horseshoe Theatre Company until it's closure and demolition in 1992. Sadly there is no trace of this building today.

Sources and Credits

Within Living Memory by Diana Stanley (1967) Published by Barrie Smith Printed by Megaron Press Ltd., Bournemouth.

London's Lost Route to Basingstoke, The story of The Basingstoke Canal by P.A.L. Vine (1994), Published by Alan Sutton Publishing Inc. 83 Washington Street, Dover. ISBN 0-7509-0228-0

The Making of Basingstoke, From Prehistory to the Present Day by Eric Stokes MA, DFC and bar (2008) published by the Basingstoke Archaeological & Historical Society. ISBN 978-0-9508095-3-3

The Illustrated History of Basingstoke by Arthur Attwood MBE (2001) Published by The Breedon Books Publishing Company Limited, Breedon House, 3 The Parker Centre, Derby, DE21 4SZ. ISBN 1-85983-271-7

A History of Overton in Hampshire from 1500 by Richard Waldram, Jane Anthony, Charles Cardiff, Janet Exley, Adrian Lewis, Valda Stevens. (2019) Published by Heritage Overton, 2019. ISBN 978-1-5272-4611-9

Basingstoke History (Facebook) site, Wikipedia, Wikipedia Commons, Basingstoke Gazette, Hants & Berks Gazette, general Internet sites.

	Chapter	*Photo credit*

1	Ruth Ellis	Ruth Ellis
		   Mirrorpix
		Ruth in her modelling days
		   Find a grave
		The grave of Ruth Ellis
		   Find a grave

2	Blue Peter Retreads	Blue Peter Retreads in the 1960s
		   Adrian Pink
		Avon Tyre Company party 1948
		   Kevin Ackland
		Blue Peter FC 1963
		   Adrian Donnelly
		The Moniton Trading estate
		   Ian Richards

		A Blue Peter promotional badge
Wikipedia
The Blue Peter Industrial Estate aerial view
Aerial Films Ltd
3	Tollgates and Milestones	Milestone marker at Kempshott
Ian Richards
A rutted road depiction of the 1700s
Wikipedia
The Toll House kiosk and The 'Round House' Tollhouse 2020
Ian Richards
Advert for a toll franchise
Wikimedia commons
4	The Salvation Army Riots	William and Catherine Booth
Wikimedia commons
Mr Sopers' house in Vyne Road
HCMS
A shop in Station Hill
Arthur Attwood
General Booth in Winton Square
Arthur Attwood
5	The Costello School	Miss Costello
The Costello school
Brook House
Unknown
The Harriot Costello school 1970
Alastair Blair
The Costello school today
Ian Richards
6	Joices Waggons	Joices yard circa 1880
Arthur Attwood
The Landau
Wikimedia commons
Joices yard 1967
Diana Stanley
7	The coaching inns	The Red Lion in the 1960s
Robert Brown
8	Education	Fairfields school 1903
Robert Brown
The British school
Sarum Hill 1880
Hampshire Cultural Trust
The Congregational Church c1900
Terry Hunt
St Johns School circa 1905
Alastair Blair

Church Cottage 1920
Alastair Blair
The Blue Coat school 1950s
HCMAS

9   Hackwood House

Hackwood House 1818
Unknown
Modern Hackwood House
Terry Redman /SWNS

10   The Haymarket Theatre

The corn exchange
Arthur Attwood
The Haymarket Theatre pre 1992
Arthur Attwood
The Lesser Market
Ian Richards
The Haymarket Theatre today
Ian Richards

11   Mr Mulford

Mulfords Hill, Tadley.
Ian Richards
The resting place of John Mulford.
Ian Richards
The grave of John Mulford.
Ian Richards

12   Local Traders

Chapel Street 1920
Terry Hunt
Tadley Besom Broom Makers
Unknown
A knife sharpener
Robert Brown

13   John May

John May
Arthur Attwood
May Street in the 1960s
Robert Brown
The May family circa 1900
Arthur Attwood

14   The Mays Brewery

Mays brewery
Robert Brown
Mays brewery Brook Street
Robert Brown
The Cricketers Inn
Robert Brown
The Goat Inn
Robert Brown

15   The Boys Brigade

The 1st Basingstoke Boys Brigade Company c 1958
Ian Richards

16	Alfie and Jessie Cole	Jesse Cole senior and daughters. *Bobby Cole* Alfie Cole and pony. *Graham photography* The Cole family at a family wedding 1950s. *Bobby Cole* The Cole caravan site, Eastrop circa 1960. *Graham photography* The Basingstoke Gas Works circa 1955. *Cathy Williams* A bender tent. *Wikipedia*
17	All Saints Church	The laying of the foundation stone 1915. *Unknown* An original design drawing. *architecture.com*
18	The 60s Pop Groups	Local group The Mimets *Robert Brown* The Troggs 1966. *Wikipedia* The Brinkletts Basingstoke Youth Centre 1964. *Ian Richards* Advertisement for the Ticky Rick club circa 1962. *Newsquest* Georgie Fame and the Blue Flames. *Wikipedia* The Pied Piper restaurant. *Newsquest* The Beatles at the Pied Piper 1967. *Wordpress.com* St Josephs hall *Robert Brown* John Finden (Johnny Prince) *Robert Brown*
19	The Sarum Hill Centre	The Sarum Hill Centre today. *Ian Richards* The centre as the Mazawattee Tea Co circa 1870. *Peter Davis* The original school floor plan circa 1841 *Peter Davis*
20	Potters Lane	The demolition of Potters Lane *Robert Brown* Charlie Everetts cycle shop. *Robert Brown* The Philpotts bakery waiting for demolition. *Robert Brown*

                    The worlds oldest wedding cake
                        Ian Richards/Basingstoke museum
                    Ruby and Winnie Philpott
                        Robert Brown
                    Potters Lane circa 1900.
                        Terry Hunt
                    Potters Lane pre 1966.
                        Robert Brown

21   The Fire Brigade   A steam powered fire tender
                                    sfbhistory.org.uk

22   The Candovers   St Marys Church, Preston Candover
                                    Ian Richards
                    The South view.
                        Ian Richards
                    The interior.
                        Ian Richards
                    The 1658 commemorate of Samuel Evans.
                        Ian Richards

23   Lancaster the   Sir James Lancaster.
       Explorer   *Wikipedia*
                    Lancaster Road.
                        Ian Richards
                    East India House London c1817.
                        Wikipedia
                    An English Galleon circa 1600.
                        Pinterest

24   Lansing Bagnall   The Isleworth works 1947.
                                  Lansing Bagnall
                    Basingstoke works Kingsclere Road 1952.
                        Lansing Bagnall
                    Product design building, Kimbell Road 1970.
                        Ian Richards

25   The Quakers   Warren House a painting 1966.
                                  Diana Stanley
                    The Quaker Meeting House 1966.
                        Diana Stanley
                    Quakers.
                        Historynet

26   Captain Susan   Captain Susan 'Hawker' Jones.
       'Hawker' Jones   *Bobby Cole*
                    The Salvation Army Temple circa 1950s.
                        Unknown
                    Mrs Bramwell Booth.
                        Wikipedia
                    Baughurst chapel today.
                        Ian Richards
                    St Stephen's Church, Baughurst.
                        Ian Richards

                    The War Cry paper obituary 14th May 1892.
                        Bobby Cole

27 King Johns castle   King Johns castle 2018
                        Ian Richards
                    King John.
                        Cassell's History of England
                    The Magna Carta 1215.
                        The British Library

28 Portals mill   Laverstoke people waiting for the royal visit.
                        Terry Hunt
                    King George V visit Portals 1923.
                        Terry Hunt
                    Overton Mill today.
                        Ian Richards

29 The Basingstoke   The plan of Basingstoke wharf
    canal   *Ian Richards*
                    The entrance to the tunnel at Greywell.
                        Ian Richards
                    Basingstoke wharf 1904.
                        P.A.L. Vine
                    * Quote: From The Illustrated History of
                    Basingstoke by Arthur Attwood.

30 The Shrubbery   The Shrubbery circa 1930.
                        Newsquest
                    The Mother and baby statue.
                        Ian Richards
                    The Shrubbery in the 1960s
                        Robert Brown

Index

Aldermaston 27
All Saints church 55, 69
Aly Khan, IV 41
    Princess Joan 41
Angel, The 31, 84
Anvil Theatre, The 45, 79
Arnold 29
Ashford Hill 16
Austen, Jane 30
Auto Tyre Services 10
Awdry, Right Rev Doctor William 70

Barbarians 22
Barge Inn, The 90
Baring, Alexander 93
Barron, Rev 21
Basing House 40
Basingstoke, Borough Council 106
    and District Hospital 135
    canal 20, 119, 121, 126
    common 24
    Community Church 82, 83
    Gazette 95
    Navigation Company 126, 130
    police 21
    society 131
    Technical College 25
    town hall 22, 23
    wharf 127
    Youth Centre 74
BATS 44
Baughurst 8, 16, 111
    Inhurst 8
Beaconsfield Road 86
Beatles, The 73, 79
Berg Estate, The 46
Berry, William 40
Besom brooms 50
Bird, John 20
Blakely, David 7, 8
Blatch W.H., Mayor 21
Blue Anchor, The 57
Blue Coat school, The 35
Blue Peter Retreads 10, 12, 13

Blue Room 74
Booth, General 19, 23, 43, 117
    Bramwell, Mrs 117
Bounty Road 53
Boy's Brigade, The 61
Bramley 8
Bradleys printing shop 8
Breweries 19
Brimpton 8
Brinkletts Centre 74
British and Foreign Bible Society 34
British Schools 34
British Workman, The 85
Brook House 24
Brook Street 20, 24, 56, 65, 110
    lower 36, 38
Broughams 29
Burberry 130, 134
Burghclere 16
Buried Church, The 91

Camrose, Viscount 41
    Lady 41
Candovers, The 91, 95
Carpenters Yard 85
Carriers 50, 51
Caston's Walk 31
Chamberlain, Neville Sir 40
Chapel Street/Hill 16, 52, 53, 55, 110
Charles II, King 112
Charles Chute school 38
Chineham 16
Churchill Way 24, 56
Churchill, Winston Sir 40. 41
Church, Street 21, 43, 69, 84
    square 21
    Cottage 35
    lower 38
Cliddesden 91
    Road 38, 90, 132
Coach lamps 27
Cole, Alfie & Jesse 64, 68, 114
Coles yard 66
Congregational Church 21, 23

Corn Exchange, The 22, 43, 90
Costello, Miss 24, 25
    school 24, 26, 38
    Technology College 26
Council school 36
Cow Cross Street 42
Crossborough Hill 24, 38
Cross Street 35, 42
Crown, The 30, 31, 126

Daily Telegraph, The 41
d'Andley, Richard 92
Destitute 8
Dogmersfield 127
Drake, Sir Francis 100
Drovers 15
Duchy of Normandy 120
Dummer 16
Dunsford Crescent 8

East India Company 100
Easter Sunday 1955 8
Eastrop 16, 24, 39
Edward Bonaventure *100*
Elizabeth I, Queen 15, 101
Elizabeth of the Belgians 40
Ellis, Ruth 7
    execution 9
    mother 8
    Andy, suicide 9
Euston Road, London 29
Everett, Charlie 85

Fairfields 36, 82
    school 8, 36
Feathers, The 31
Financial Times 40
Finden, John 74
Five Mile Act, The 112
Flaxfield Road 38
Fox, George 111

Galaxy Club, The 74
Gas works 65
Gazette, Basingstoke *20*
    Hants & Berks *20, 23, 110*
George, The 31
George I, King 40
George V, King 124

George VI, King 124
Giddy, Davies MP 33
Goat, The 57
Goat Lane 57
Grand (exchange) theatre, The 7, 43
Greywell 126, 128, 131
Gypsies 52

Hackwood Road 16
    Estate 39, 65
    House 39, 40
Hail the Conquering Heroes 22
Hampshire Brick & Tile Co 129, 131
Harrow Way 46
Hartley Wespall 56
Haymarket theatre, The 7, 42, 43, 45, 54, 75, 90
Hibberd, Superintendent 21
High school, The Girl's 24, 38
Hinton, Miss 24
Holloway prison 9
Holy Ghost, school 46
Hornby, Athur 7
    Bertha 8
Horseshoe Theatre Company 135
House of Commons 22

I'm All Right Jack 107

Jack, Sister Jessie 134
Jacob's yard 27
Joice, John & Son 27, 30
    Arnold 27
Jones, Susan 'Hawker' 114
Jordan, Captain 20

KATT cup, The 12
Kaye, Sir Emmanual 108
Kelvin Engineering 12
Kempshott 16
King John's castle 119
Kingsclere 27, 112
Kings school, The 34

Lancaster, Sir James 100, 101
Lancaster Road 100
Landowners 15
Lansing Bagnall Ltd 104
Lansing Linde 108

143

Laverstoke Mill 122
Lesser Market 43, 54
Loddon, river 20, 64
London 8, 27
    street 30, 32
    Road 34

Magdela public house 8
Magna Carta, The 120, 121
Mapledurwell 16
Market square 20, 27
Massaganians 22, 23, 114
    Slingo 22
May, John (Lt Col) 53, 56, 60, 71, 133
    Bounty 53
    brewery 20
    place 53
    Street 69, 70
    Thomas & William 57
Memorial park 16
Moniton estate 10, 13
Monk Sherborne 8
Mortimer Common 48
Movies, silent 7
    sound 8
Mulford, John 46, 48
    Hill 46

National
    school 35
    Society 34
Neilson, Arthur 7
Newnham 16
New Road 43
Norn Hill 116
North Waltham 114

Oakley 16
Odiham 119, 127
Old Basing 64
Ote Street 43
Overton 16, 122
    mill 123

Pamber 16
    forest 50, 52
Park Prewett 8
Parliament, bill 15
Paulet, William 40

Pegasus 107
Phillip II of France 120
Philpotts 86
Pied Piper restaurant 79
Pinkerton 128
Poole 27
Portals 122, 123
Post Office, The 90
Potters Lane 84, 85, 87
Prince, Johnny 74
Pubs 19

Quaker, Charles Heath 109, 110
Queen Elizabeth II 124
Queen Mary's school 25, 38, 54

Radford Potter, Dr 44
Reading 27
Reading Road 16, 69
Red Lion Inn, The 8, 31
Religious Society of Friends 109
Richard I, King 119
Richard Aldworth 35
Riot, Act 22
Romany Gypsy 114
Rose & Crown, The 84
Rotherwick 126
Royal Horse Artillery, The 22

Salisbury 27, 30
    Cathedral 121
    Flying Machine, The 30
Salvation Army, The 19, 23, 43, 115, 117
Sarum Hill 30, 61, 80, 82
    Centre 34, 80
    Domestic Science Centre 25
School Board, The 35, 36
Sherborne St John 132
Sherfield on Loddon 8
Shetland pony carriage 29
Ship, The 57
Shooters Way 38
Shrubbery, Girls school 25
    Maternity Home 132
Silk Mill, Old 20, 21, 23
Silver Star restaurant 85
Soper, Grove 36
    Mr 23

Southern Counties Cycle Co 85
Southern Road 55
South Ham 46
South View cemetery 16, 46
St Andrews Church 62
St John's, hospital 38
    school 38
St Michaels Church 69, 70
Stag & Hounds 79
Stokes family 8
Sunday Times 40

Tadley, 46, 111
    Newtown 8
Temperance movement 23
Thornycrofts 12, 69
Three Mariners, The 31
Three Tuns, The 57
Ticky Rick club 74
Tollgates and Milestones 14, 17
    franchises 15
    mileways 15
    toll houses 15, 16
Top of The Town 31
Trinity Methodist Church, The 62
Troggs, The 74
Turnpikes 15, 16, 17
Twist & Trad 74
Tylney Hall 126
Tyres, retread 10

URC, church 21, 34

Victoria Street 57, 70
Vyne Rd 23
    school 38

Waggons 15, 16, 17, 27. 27, 30
Warren House 109
Webber's garage 30
Wedding cake, The Worlds oldest 86
Western Way 62
Weston, Mr & Mrs 25
Wheatsheaf, The 30
Whitburn, John 47
Whitchurch 122
William Alexander Smith, Sir 61
William III, King 15
Willis museum 31, 54, 67

Wilson, PM Harold 67
Winchester 27
    prison 22
    road 79
    street 27, 29, 30, 32, 57, 74
Windover Street 30, 114
Winton Square 30, 36
Woodman, George 20
Worting 10, 16
    Road 110
Wote Street 7, 20, 31, 43, 54, 57, 84, 85, 90, 109, 127